KS1 M... ...ion Guide

...nt

Welcome to the magical world of Wizard Whimstaff – a wise wizard with great Maths powers!

Whimstaff wants to pass on his powers to you. He has some friends to help him.

Miss Snufflebeam – a forgetful young dragon who is always getting confused...

Pointy – Whimstaff's smart goblin assistant...

And Mugly and Bugly – Pointy's lazy pet frogs, who prefer eating and snoozing to learning, but still have a few tricks to teach you.

Just work your way through the pages of this book and you too will become a real Maths wizard like Wizard Whimstaff and his friends!

Good luck, young wizard!

Letts

Contents

Numbers

tick when completed

Calculations

Shapes and measures

Handling data

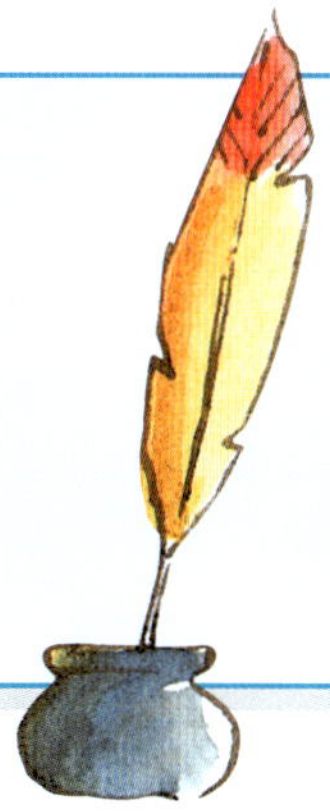

Counting

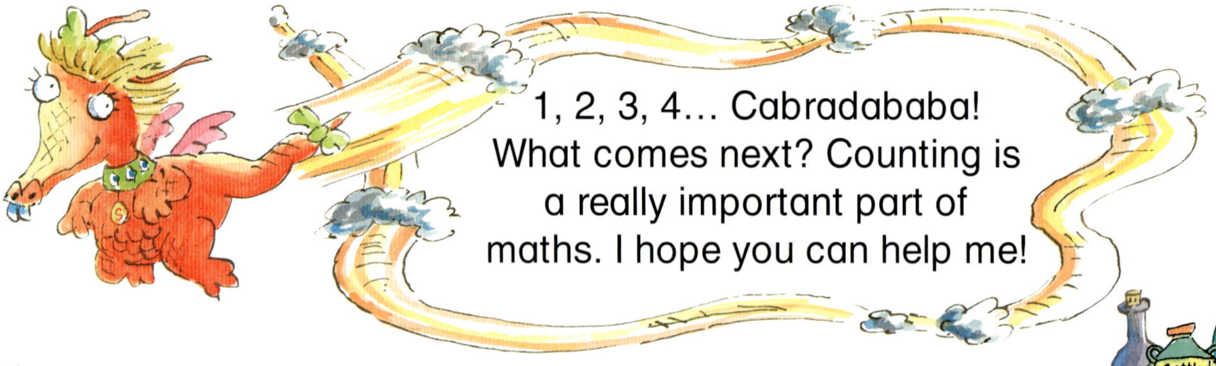

Counting objects is fun!

Help! This looks like a lot of bugs to count. Can you count them for me? Make sure you do not miss any out!

Did you count 20 bugs? Oh well done!

Now can you count them in twos? 2, 4, 6, 8, 10, 12…
This can be a lot quicker.

You are so clever! Now you might even be able to count in groups of five! 5, 10, 15, 20…

Are you a good estimator?

Estimating is such a big word. It is like guessing, but it is better than a guess if you are good with numbers.

Have a quick look at this pile of buttons. Without counting, estimate roughly how many you think there are.

Was your estimate between 10 and 20? Now count them to see how good your 'guesstimate' was!

Can you count to 100?

You need to know the numbers to 100.

Use this number grid to help you learn the positions of all the numbers. You will be as clever as Wizard Whimstaff soon!

0	1	2	3	4	5	6	7	8	9
10	11	12	13	14	15	16	17	18	19
20	21	22	23	24	25	26	27	28	29
30	31	32	33	34	35	36	37	38	39
40	41	42	43	44	45	46	47	48	49
50	51	52	53	54	55	56	57	58	59
60	61	62	63	64	65	66	67	68	69
70	71	72	73	74	75	76	77	78	79
80	81	82	83	84	85	86	87	88	89
90	91	92	93	94	95	96	97	98	99

Use the tens to help you read the numbers. For example, 26 is 20 + 6. So, to find 26, go down to 20 and then across to 26.

MAGIC WORDS: estimate

Wizard's Practice

Workbook pages 4-5

1. Estimate the number of spots on the ladybird.
2. Count the spots to check your estimate. How many spots are there?
3. How many spots would there be if there was 1 more?
4. What number comes after 38?
5. What number comes before 70?

Digits and numbers

Hey presto! You need to learn how to read, write and use all the numbers to 99. The good news is that you only need to learn how to use 10 digits for this!

Read, write and learn your numbers!

Numbers are all around us, young wizard. Look out for them and, most importantly, learn how to read and write them.

Here are the numbers from 0 to 9.

0	1	2	3	4	5	6	7	8	9
zero	one	two	three	four	five	six	seven	eight	nine

Practise writing each number, so that you become quick and skilful.

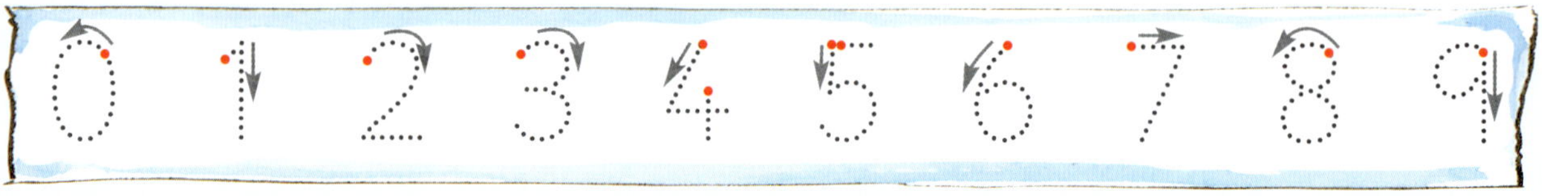

Now try the numbers to 20.

The numbers between 10 and 20 can seem strange. You say them in a different way to the other numbers, so read these and make sure you know how to say each one out loud.

10 ten	11 eleven	12 twelve	13 thirteen	14 fourteen	15 fifteen
16 sixteen	17 seventeen	18 eighteen	19 nineteen	20 twenty	

Can you see the 'teen' numbers? Teenagers are aged between 13 and 19 years old.

Use two digits to make different numbers!

Allakazan! It is amazing that all our numbers are made from just 10 **digits**.

0 1 2 3 4 5 6 7 8 9

The position of these digits in a number makes each number different.

34	52
Thirty-four This is 3 'tens' and 4 'ones', or 30 + 4.	Fifty-two This is 5 'tens' and 2 'ones', or 50 + 2.

These are 2-digit numbers. Remember, the first digit shows the tens.

10 20 30 40 50 60 70 80 90

When you read a 2-digit number, it helps to break it up into tens and ones.

MAGIC WORDS: **digit**

Wizard's Practice

Workbook pages 6-7

1. Write the number 14 as a word. ____________________
2. Write eighteen as a number. [ ]
3. What number does the abacus show? [ ]
4. 60 + 5 = [ ]
5. What number is ten more than 38? [ ]

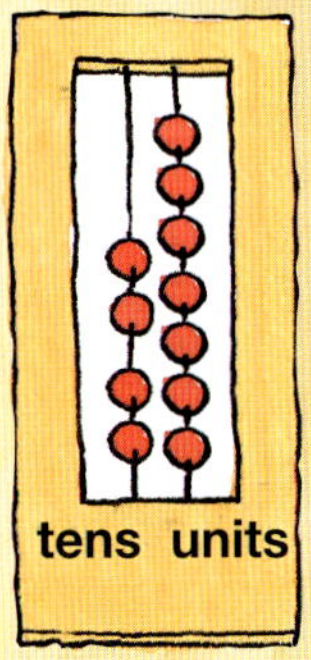

Special numbers

Numbers are super, because they have so many patterns! Look out for special numbers too, because they do magical things!

All numbers are either odd or even.

These are the **odd** and **even numbers** to 20.

Remember that odd numbers always end in 1, 3, 5, 7 or 9 and even numbers always end in 0, 2, 4, 6 or 8. It is easy when you know how!

Odd Numbers	Even Numbers
1	2
3	4
5	6
7	8
9	10
11	12
13	14
15	16
17	18
19	20

Even numbers can be **divided** exactly into groups of 2. Odd numbers cannot be divided into groups of 2, there is always 1 left over.

Zero is nothing really!

0, or **zero**, is a special number with lots of other names too, like **nothing**, **nought** and **nil**. Zero is used in different ways, for example:

All the cakes have been eaten, so there are 0 cakes left.

10, 20, 30, 40, 50 … all end in 0 to show they have no 'ones'.

If you have to add zero to a number or take away zero from a number, remember that the number does not change. You will soon get the hang of it!

7 + 0 = 7   4 – 0 = 4

Patterns are super!

I like counting patterns in different steps.

To work out the steps in a **sequence**, look at the **difference** between the numbers.

17 19 21 23 25 ?

The difference between each number is 2, so the next number is 2 more, which is 27. Super!

Did you recognise that those were odd numbers? Now look at this sequence:

30 40 50 60 70 ?

The difference between each number is 10, so the next number is 10 more, which is 80.

To help work out the missing numbers in a sequence, draw 'jumps' between each number and write the differences over each jump.

2 2 2 2

14 16 18 ____ 22

MAGIC WORDS

odd number • even number • divide
zero • sequence • difference

Wizard's Practice

Workbook pages 8-9

1. Is 21 an even or odd number? ____________
2. Is 30 an even or odd number? ____________
3. What is the answer if zero is added to 15? ☐
4. What is the missing number in these sequences?

7 9 ☐ 13 15 17	30 28 26 ☐ 22 20

Comparing and ordering

Brain cell alert! You need to be able to compare numbers and put them in order.

First, second, third... last!

Pointy is always trying to come first. We are always too busy eating. Slurp!

Numbers with **st**, **th**, **rd** or **nd** written after them can look strange. They show the order or position of things. Look at these and try to remember each one:

1st first	2nd second	3rd third	4th fourth	5th fifth
6th sixth	7th seventh	8th eighth	9th ninth	10th tenth

Large or small? Compare to check!

Croak! When you need to compare two numbers, you must look carefully at the digits. You may want to find the largest or smallest.

Which is larger, 45 or 54?

45 is the same as 40 + 5.
54 is the same as 50 + 4.
54 is larger than 45.

If you are unsure, use a 100-square or a number line to help you compare numbers or put them in order.

Equal and not equal!

The symbols = < and > are really useful. Try to learn what each one does. Slurp!

= means ‘is equal to’.
4 + 8 = 12

< means ‘is less than’ 38 < 42
38 is less than 42.

> means ‘is greater than’ 27 > 18
27 is greater than 18.

Now learn to order numbers. Slurp!

Is this anything to do with ordering food? When you put numbers in order of size, order the **tens** to start with, then order the **ones**.

Try this. Can you put these numbers in order, starting with the smallest?

38 36 63 41 29

Use these two simple steps.

1st step Look at the **tens** and write them in order: 29, 38, 36, 41, 63.

2nd step If any of the **tens** are the same, put the **ones** in order: 29, 36, 38, 41, 63.

Always look carefully at the question when you put numbers in order. Do you need to start with the smallest number or the largest number?

MAGIC WORDS equal

Wizard's Practice

Workbook pages 10-11

1. The first star is green. What colour is the 4th star? ________
2. Which number is bigger, 37 or 73? ☐
3. Use one of the signs = < or > to make this correct: 38 ☐ 19
4. Write a number between 20 and 30 to make this correct: 26 < ☐
5. Write these numbers in order, starting with the smallest. 26 30 18 34 51 ☐ ☐ ☐ ☐ ☐

Number lines and tracks

There are so many numbers! Number lines and number tracks are very useful to help learn the order of numbers.

Number lines are lines of numbers.

Abracadada! Some number lines have all the numbers written on them. You can compare numbers on this number line.

Oops! Some lines have numbers missing. You need to look at the numbers and the markers to work them out.

This arrow points to 29. It is 1 less than 30 and 4 more than 25. My head hurts!

Blank number lines have numbers missing.

This number line has only got the start and finish numbers. How can you work out what number the arrow points to?

You need to ***estimate*** *the number. So this number is bigger than 25 and smaller than 50. Do you estimate it to be about 30? You are clever!*

There are number tracks and grids too.

I am not very good at counting, but number tracks help.

60	61	62	63	64	65	66	67	68	69	70	71

Oh dear! This grid looks more difficult. Where is the number 21 going to be?

Look at the pattern and count. It just goes below the 15! So where does 28 go?

6	7	8	9	10	11
12	13	14	15	16	

Number grids are a bit like number tracks put into rows. Look at the last number in a row and the first number in the next row to see that it is like a single track.

Halfway points are between two numbers.

You might be asked to find a number halfway between two others on a number line. What number is halfway between 7 and 15?

Wizard Whimstaff has a clever way of finding halfway numbers. Add up the two end numbers and then halve the answer. That will be the middle number!

$$7 + 15 = 22$$

***Half** of 22 is 11. 11 is halfway between 7 and 15. Clever!*

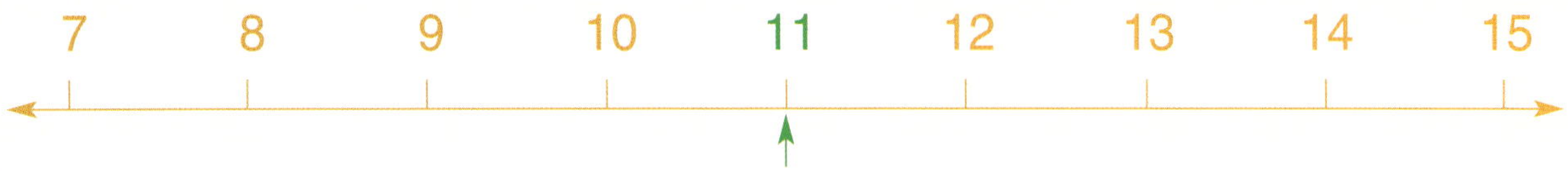

MAGIC WORDS

estimate • half

Wizard's Practice

Workbook pages 12-13

1. What number is the arrow pointing to?

2. Fill in the missing number on the number track.

55	56	57	58	59	60		62	63	64	65

Fractions

Fractions are such fun! Just remember that fractions are equal parts of a whole. Halves and quarters are the ones to think about. You will soon get the hang of it!

A half is one part out of two equal parts.

If you cut any shape into 2 equal parts, you are cutting it into halves.

I need to share a cake equally between Mugly and Bugly, so I need to cut the cake in half. Super!

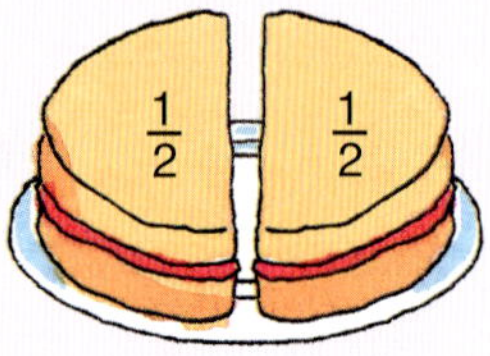

*Half is written as $\frac{1}{2}$ to show that it is in 2 **equal** parts.*

Not half

Half

Check that a shape is in 2 equal parts for it to be in half.

A quarter is one part out of four equal parts.

If you cut any shape into 4 equal parts, you are cutting it into quarters.

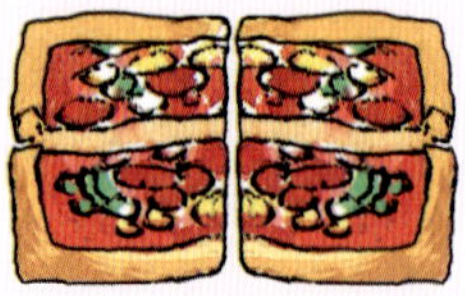

One-quarter is written as $\frac{1}{4}$ to show it is in 4 equal parts.

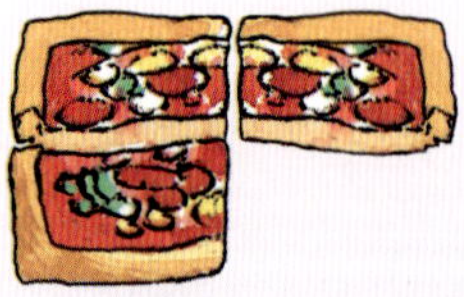

So if you want to eat $\frac{1}{4}$ of a pizza, you can cut the pizza into four pieces and take one of the pieces. This leaves $\frac{3}{4}$ (three quarters) for your friends to eat.

This red shape is not in quarters. It is in four parts, but the parts are not equal. Shapes cut into quarters are in four **equal** parts.

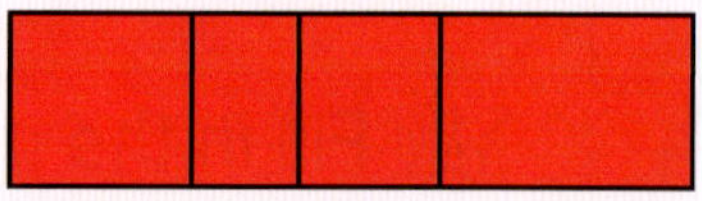

Fractions of amounts are super!

If you want to share things equally, you need to **divide** them.

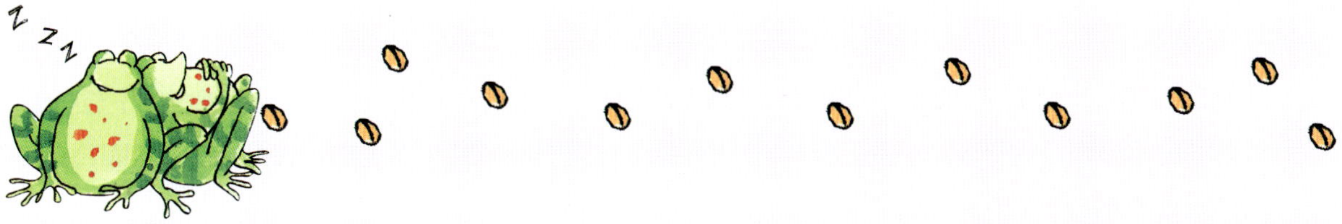

I want to share these seeds between Mugly and Bugly. There are 12 seeds, so divide them by 2 and Mugly and Bugly each get 6 seeds.

What if Miss Snufflebeam and Wizard Whimstaff also want some seeds? I will need to divide the seeds between 4 to find $\frac{1}{4}$ of 12.

$\frac{1}{2}$ of 12 = 6

$\frac{1}{4}$ of 12 = 3

MAGIC WORDS fraction • equal • divide

Wizard's Practice

Workbook pages 14-15

1. What fraction of the circle is blue? ________

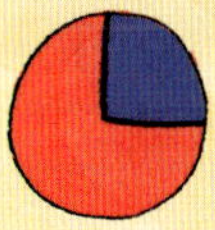

2. Circle the shape that shows $\frac{1}{2}$.

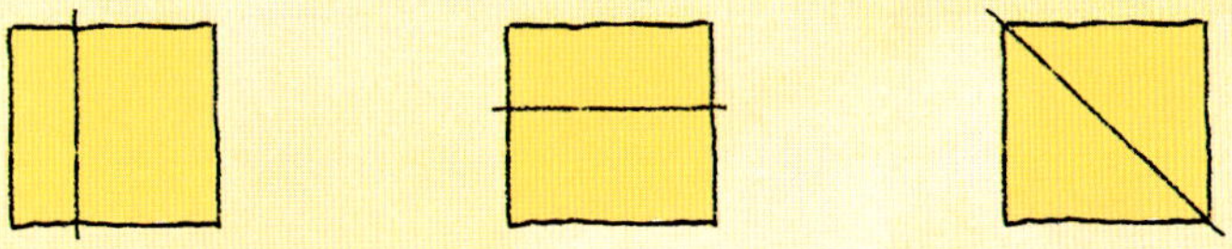

3. Draw a circle round half of these balls.

4. What is $\frac{1}{2}$ of 14? ☐
5. What is $\frac{1}{4}$ of 20? ☐

Wizard's Challenge

1 Counting

Brain cell alert! Estimate how many bugs there are in each group and write down your guess. Then count the bugs and write down how many there really are.

a  Estimate ☐ Actual amount ☐

b  Estimate ☐ Actual amount ☐

c  Estimate ☐ Actual amount ☐

d  Estimate ☐ Actual amount ☐

2 Digits and numbers

Well done, slurp! Now write the missing numbers for each of these.

a 50 + 1 = ☐

b 10 + ☐ = 19

c ☐ + 2 = 82

d 60 + 3 = ☐

3 Special numbers

Sequences make us sleepy. Fill in these missing numbers for us while we have a snooze.

a ☐ 36 38 ☐ 42 44

b 58 59 60 ☐ 62 ☐

c 70 ☐ 50 ☐ 30 20

d 25 28 ☐ 34 37 ☐

4 Comparing and ordering

Burp! Bug biscuits. Yum, yum! Draw a circle round the largest number in each set.

a 37 17 97 47

b 81 86 84 89

c 56 66 55 65

d 92 39 93 29

e 88 18 80 81

5 Number lines and tracks

Burp! Estimate the number each arrow points to.

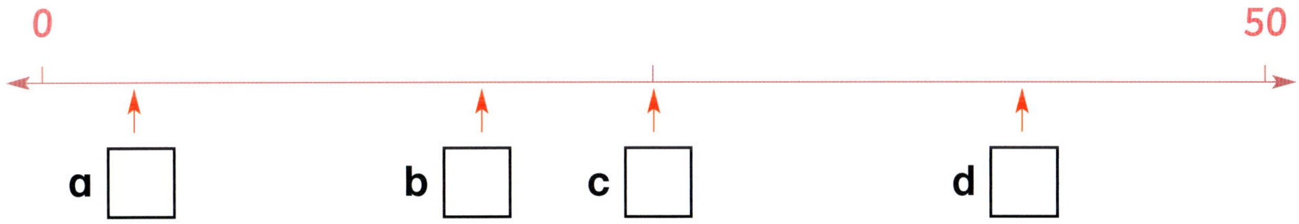

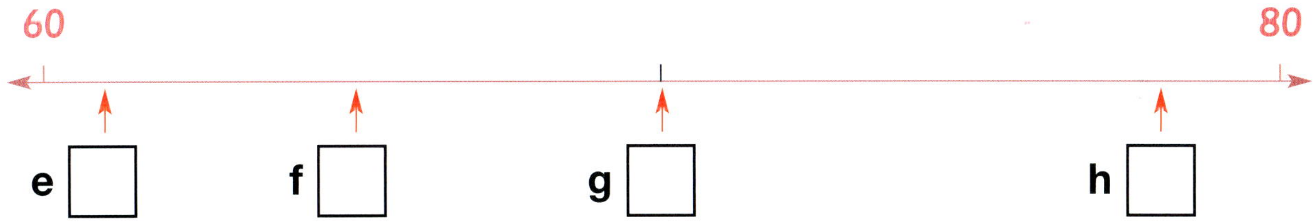

6 Fractions

Time for a snack! Halve or quarter these amounts for us.

a 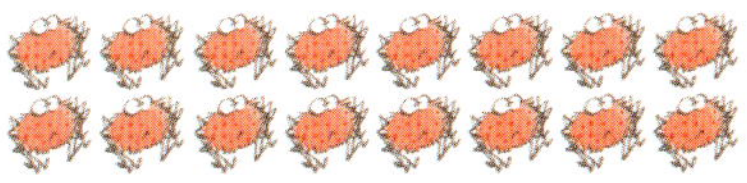 $\frac{1}{2}$ of 16 is ____

b  $\frac{1}{4}$ of 8 is ____

c  $\frac{1}{4}$ of 20 is ____

Addition

There are lots of different ways to add numbers together, young wizard. If you want to be a maths wizard, then make sure you practise these.

Put things together to add sets.

Allakazan! When you put sets of objects together, you are adding them. The sign for adding is **+**.

6 + 5 = 11
6 add 5 equals 11.
The **total** of 6 and 5 is 11.

4 + 5 + 7 = 16
4 add 5 add 7 equals 16.
The total of 4, 5 and 7 is 16.

Remember, it does not matter which number you add first. 6 + 5 and 5 + 6 both total 11.

Add by counting on.

Use a number line to help make adding easier.

What is 15 + 7? Start at 15 and count on 7. 15 + 7 = 22

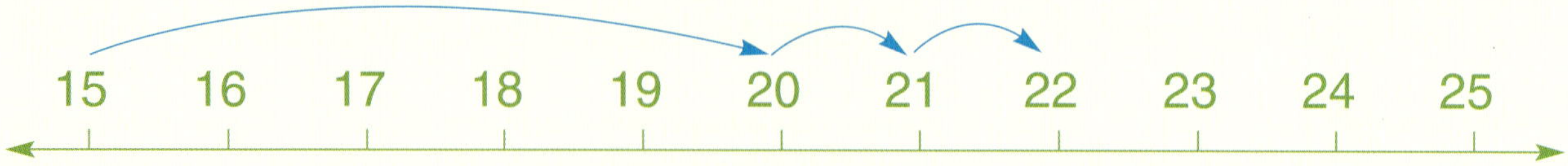

A quick way is to count on from 15 to 20 in a big jump of 5, and then count on 2.

Counting on from the bigger number is quicker. To work out 23+6, count on from 23 not 6.

Allakazan! You can add in tens too.

If you know a fact such as 4 + 2 = 6, you can use this to work out other additions.

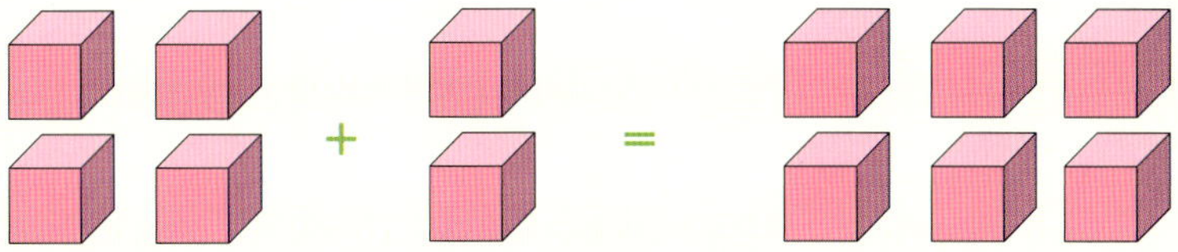

4 + 2 = 6

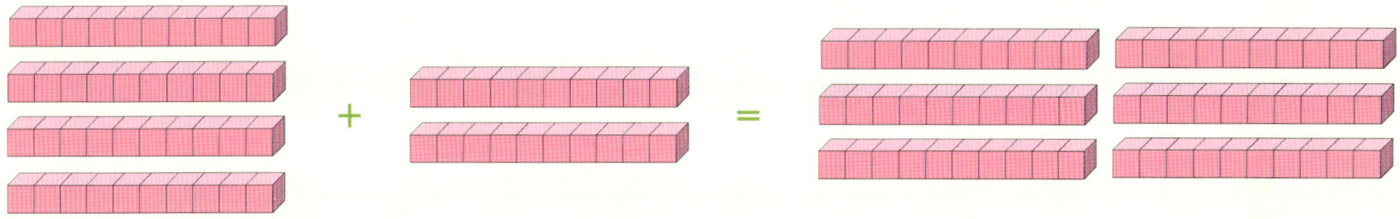

4 tens + 2 tens = 6 tens
40 + 20 = 60

Now wave your wand and use the above to help you work out 43 + 20.

43 is the same as 40 + 3.

40 + 3 + 20 is the same as 40 + 20 + 3, which is 63.

MAGIC WORDS: total

Wizard's Practice

Workbook pages 16-17

1. What is the total of 5, 8 and 3? ☐
2. What is 6 more than 18? ☐
3. 30 + ☐ = 37
4. 40 + 30 = ☐
5. 26 + 40 = ☐

Subtraction

Subtraction seems like such a hard word! I must remember that it just means take away, which is the opposite of add.

Taking away makes things disappear!

Cabradababa! This is a magic take away pot. It always takes away 2.

I put in 6 spiders and when I look again there are only 4.

6 – 2 = 4

I put in 7 and only 5 come out.

7 – 2 = 5

Adding is the opposite of taking away. Adding puts all the spiders back into the pot.

6 – 2 = 4 4 + 2 = 6 7 – 2 = 5 5 + 2 = 7

Remember, the subtraction sign looks like this: –

Counting back to take away!

This is a clever idea from Pointy. If you want to take away one number from another, count back on a number track.

What is 18 – 5? Start at 18 and count back 5. 18 – 5 = 13

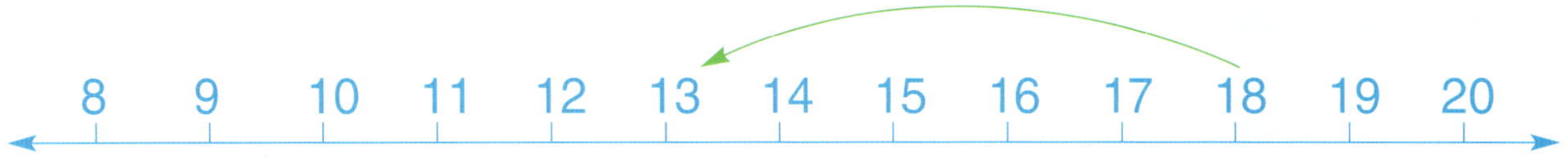

Differences are something to count on!

Pointy says that a really good way to subtract is to find the **difference** between the numbers. He counts on from the lower number.

What is the difference between 18 and 25?

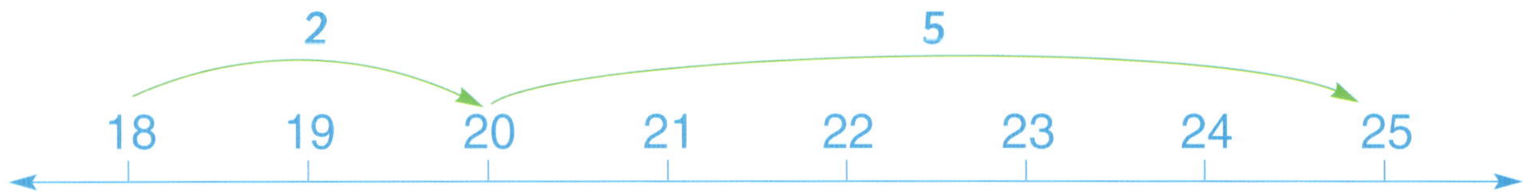

This number line shows exactly what goes on in your head.

Start at 18, add on 2 to 20 and add on 5 more to 25.

2 + 5 = 7   So 25 – 18 = 7

Finding the difference by counting on is a good method when two numbers are close together. Look at the numbers carefully to choose the best method, counting on or counting back.

MAGIC WORDS subtract • difference

Wizard's Practice

Workbook pages 18-19

1. What is 28 take away 5? ☐
2. 17 – ☐ = 13
3. 40 – 10 = ☐
4. What is the difference between 28 and 31? ☐
5. What is 8 less than 20? ☐

Multiplication

Now, young wizard, let me tell you about magnificent multiplication. It is a quick and useful way to count groups.

Multiplying is just counting groups!

Allakazan! Multiplication is the same as adding groups again and again. Let me show you by counting these groups of spiders.

There are 4 spiders in each jar. How many spiders are there altogether? We shall add the groups and find out!

Hey presto! 3 lots of 4 is the same as $4 + 4 + 4$, which is 12.

So 4 multiplied by 3 is 12.
$4 \times 3 = 12$

Do you think that 4 lots of 3 is the same as 3 lots of 4? Count the groups and see!

Dabracadabra! The answer is exactly the same, but the spiders have more room to wriggle in!

So 3 multiplied by 4 is 12.
$3 \times 4 = 12$

The multiply sign looks like this: x

Put things in columns and rows.

If we put all the wriggly little spiders together, we can see how multiplication works.

There are 3 **rows** of 4 spiders.
$4 + 4 + 4 = 12$

There are 4 **columns** of 3 spiders.
$3 + 3 + 3 + 3 = 12$

You can count the columns or the rows and the answer is the same.

$4 \times 3 = 12 \qquad 3 \times 4 = 12$

With multiplication, the answers are the same written both ways.
$4 \times 3 = 3 \times 4 \quad 5 \times 2 = 2 \times 5 \quad 3 \times 10 = 10 \times 3$

Try repeated addition on a number line.

The number line is so useful. Look how it shows a multiplication pattern by adding the same amount each time.

0 1 2 3 4 5 6 7 8 9 10 11 12 13 14 15 16 17 18 19 20

$2 + 2 + 2 + 2 + 2 + 2 + 2 = 14 \qquad 2 \times 7 = 14$

Can you use this to work out 2×9?

MAGIC WORDS: row • column

Wizard's Practice

Workbook pages 20-21

1. What is 3 groups of 5? ☐
2. $4 + 4 + 4 =$ ☐ $\times$ ☐ $=$ ☐
3. $8 \times 2 =$ ☐
4. If there are 4 stickers in a packet, how many would there be in 4 packets? ☐
5. $3 \times 5 =$ ☐

Division

Can you help me understand division? I know it is to do with sharing and grouping, but I still get confused sometimes!

Dividing is just like sharing!

Dividing can be quite tricky, but it helps if you think of it as **sharing**.

I have 15 chocolate flies to share between me, Mugly and Bugly. So how many do we get each?

15 shared between 3 is 5 each.

So $15 \div 3 = 5$

Oh no! Now Pointy and Wizard Whimstaff want some. So what is 15 divided by 5? Can you help me share them out again?

Abracadada! 15 shared between 5 gives us 3 flies each.

So $15 \div 5 = 3$

The divide sign looks like this: ÷

Dividing is also like grouping!

Sharing out 1 fly at a time is a bit slow. Wizard Whimstaff says that it is much better to **group**. Can you help me?

What is 20 flies divided by 5? 20 ÷ 5 = ?

If I was sharing, I would share out 20 flies between 5, giving 1 fly at a time.

As I am grouping, I take away 5 flies at a time until I have used all 20 flies. Then I count the number of groups.

There are 4 groups, so 20 ÷ 5 = 4

Check by multiplying. 4 groups of 5 make 20. Oh, well done!

Grouping is a good method, because the number you are dividing by tells you how many is in each group.

MAGIC WORDS divide

Wizard's Practice

Workbook pages 22-23

1. What is 16 divided by 4? ☐
2. 14 nuts are shared equally between 2 squirrels. How many does each get? ☐
3. 30 ÷ 5 = ☐
4. 20 children sit at tables in groups of 4. How many groups will there be? ☐
5. Some children share 12 grapes. Each child gets 3 grapes. How many children are there? ☐

Addition and subtraction facts

Learn all the facts to 10.

Practice makes perfect! Try to learn all these facts for the different **totals**. Use these four super steps to help you.

Step 1 Look at them.
Step 2 Cover them up.
Step 3 Say the facts.
Step 4 Check the facts.

1	2	3	4	5	6	7	8	9
0 + 1	0 + 2	0 + 3	0 + 4	0 + 5	0 + 6	0 + 7	0 + 8	0 + 9
	1 + 1	1 + 2	1 + 3	1 + 4	1 + 5	1 + 6	1 + 7	1 + 8
			2 + 2	2 + 3	2 + 4	2 + 5	2 + 6	2 + 7
					3 + 3	3 + 4	3 + 5	3 + 6
							4 + 4	4 + 5

Remember that 3 + 6 gives the same answer as 6 + 3.

Learn your number bonds to 10 and 20.

Try to learn all your **number bonds** that add to 10 and to 20. These are the addition facts that total 10 and total 20. It is easy when you know how!

= 10		= 20	
0 + 10	3 + 7	0 + 20	5 + 15
1 + 9	4 + 6	1 + 19	6 + 14
2 + 8	5 + 5	2 + 18	7 + 13
		3 + 17	8 + 12
		4 + 16	9 + 11
			0 + 10

Trios are 3 numbers for adding and subtracting.

Trios are terrific! They help you to learn your number facts. Super!

8 – 5 = 3 is a subtraction fact. The subtraction facts to 10 are easy to remember if you know your addition facts.

These are two addition facts

$3 + 5 = 8 \qquad 5 + 3 = 8$

and you can use them to work out two subtraction facts.

$8 - 5 = 3 \qquad 8 - 3 = 5$

The three numbers 8, 5 and 3 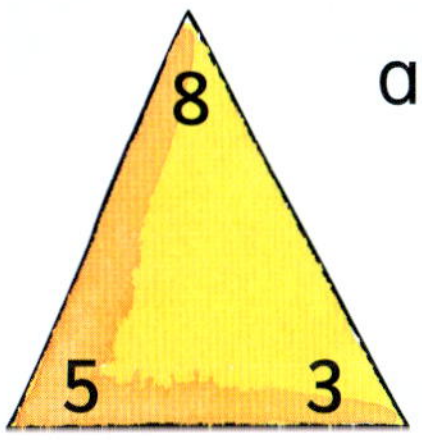 are called a trio.

They can make four addition and subtraction facts.

Think of some more trios and the facts you can make from them. You will soon get the hang of it!

Use trios to help work out missing number problems, e.g. ? – 4 = 5
If you know that 5 + 4 = 9, then you can work out that 9 – 4 = 5.
The trio is 4, 5 and 9.

MAGIC WORDS total • number bond

Wizard's Practice

Workbook pages 24-25

Try and answer these as quickly as you can.

1. 3 + 6 = ☐
2. 4 + 4 = ☐
3. 7 – 5 = ☐
4. 9 – 2 = ☐
5. 12 + 8 = ☐

Times tables

Brain cell alert! Knowing your times tables is really important. Concentrate on the 2×, 5× and 10× tables, and then you will be able to move on to the rest.

Know your doubles!

Croak! All the numbers in the 2 times table are **even numbers**.

Here is the full set up to 2×10. Can you see that they are all **doubles**?

$2 \times 1 = 2$
$2 \times 2 = 4$
$2 \times 3 = 6$
$2 \times 4 = 8$
$2 \times 5 = 10$
$2 \times 6 = 12$
$2 \times 7 = 14$
$2 \times 8 = 16$
$2 \times 9 = 18$
$2 \times 10 = 20$

They look easy when they are written in order like this, but you need to know each of these facts off by heart.

Write down any that you are not sure of and try to learn them.

Use other facts to help you. For example, if you cannot remember that 2×6 is 12, just say 2×5 is 10 and 2 more is 12.

Remember that 2×6 gives the same answer as 6×2. It does not matter which way round it is written.

To multiply by 5 and 10, look for 5s and 0s.

Slurp! These are the easiest tables to learn, because of their patterns.

Numbers in the 5× table always end in 5 or 0.

5 × 1 = 5	5 × 6 = 30
5 × 2 = 10	5 × 7 = 35
5 × 3 = 15	5 × 8 = 40
5 × 4 = 20	5 × 9 = 45
5 × 5 = 25	5 × 10 = 50

Numbers in the 10× table always end in 0.

1 × 10 = 10	6 × 10 = 60
2 × 10 = 20	7 × 10 = 70
3 × 10 = 30	8 × 10 = 80
4 × 10 = 40	9 × 10 = 90
5 × 10 = 50	10 × 10 = 100

Did you notice that when it is 5 times an **odd number**, the answer ends in 5, and when it is 5 times an even number, the answer ends in 0? Well done!

Cover each answer up with your finger. Are there any that you do not know really quickly?

15, 5 and 3 are a special set of numbers called a trio. You can use these to learn multiplication and division facts.

3 × 5 = 15   15 ÷ 5 = 3   5 × 3 = 5   15 ÷ 3 = 5

Have you noticed how multiplying and dividing are opposites?

MAGIC WORDS: even number • double • odd number

Wizard's Practice

Workbook pages 26-27

Answer these as quickly as you can.

1. 4 × 5 = ☐
2. 8 × 2 = ☐
3. 10 × 7 = ☐
4. 5 × 6 = ☐
5. 2 × 9 = ☐

Doubling and halving

It is very important to be able to **double** and **halve** numbers. I do this all the time in my spells, so work hard to learn this young wizard!

Doubles are double the fun!

Allakazan! This doubling machine is splendid. I put in any number and it magically doubles. Do you see how each number is multiplied by 2? This is the same as doubling really.

Now, learn these doubles.

1 + 1 = 2	6 + 6 = 12
2 + 2 = 4	7 + 7 = 14
3 + 3 = 6	8 + 8 = 16
4 + 4 = 8	9 + 9 = 18
5 + 5 = 10	10 + 10 = 20

Use doubles to work out near-doubles.

Splendid work! With practice, doubles of numbers can be easy to remember. If you want to be really clever, use them to work out other near-doubles.

4 + 4 = 8
4 + 5 is 1 more, which is 9.

6 + 6 = 12
6 + 7 is 1 more, which is 13.

7 + 7 = 14
7 + 8 is 1 more, which is 15.

Halving is just cutting into two parts.

Hey presto! It is easy to find one half of a number, as long as you know how to **divide** by 2. Remember that half can be written as $\frac{1}{2}$.

Here are 12 stars.

To find $\frac{1}{2}$ of 12, divide the stars into two equal groups and count one of the groups.

So $\frac{1}{2}$ of $12 = 12 \div 2 = 6$

Halving is the opposite of doubling. Half of 12 is 6. Double 6 is 12.

MAGIC WORDS: double • halve
divide

Wizard's Practice

Workbook pages 28-29

1. What is double 7? ☐
2. What is half of 20? ☐
3. $4 + 4 =$ ☐
4. $\frac{1}{2}$ of $16 =$ ☐
5. $5 + 6 =$ ☐

Solving problems

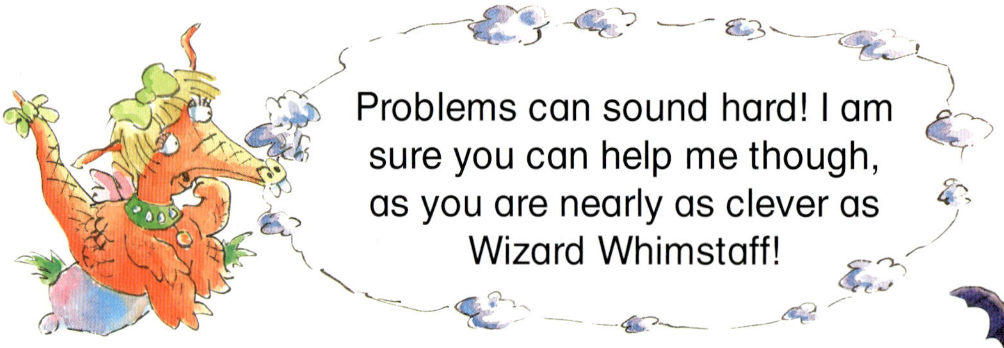

Word problems solved in 4 easy steps!

Dabracababra! Some questions are disguised as tricky word problems. When you see one, just follow the four steps.

When Dan was 3 years old, Ella was 8 years old. Now Dan is 9 years old, how old is Ella?

Step 1 Read the problem. Try to picture the problem and imagine it in real life.

Step 2 Sort out the calculations. This is one way:
Work out the difference between 3 and 9 to see how much older Dan is now, then add this to Ella's age.

Step 3 Answer the calculations. $9 - 3 = 6$ $8 + 6 = 14$

Step 4 Answer the problem. Look back at the question.
What is it asking?

Answer: Ella is now 14 years old.

Read word problems carefully to see if you need to add, take away, multiply or divide. Look out for the words that can help you decide.

Money totals – it all adds up!

Some problems ask you to add coins. Pointy says, when you are finding **totals** of a set of **coins**, always start with the highest-value coins first. Then you can add the smallest coins.

Find the total:
20p + 10p + 2p + 2p + 1p = 35p

Giving change by counting on.

Cabradababa! When shopkeepers give change, they count on from the cost of the item up to the amount of money given.

This apple costs 14p. What change will there be from 20p?

14p up to 15p is 1p   *15p up to 20p is 5p*

So the change given is 1p + 5p, which is 6p.

MAGIC WORDS: total • coin

Wizard's Practice

Workbook pages 30-31

1. There are 5 apples in a pack. How many apples are there in 3 packs?
2. Anna has 11 pens. 5 of them are black, 4 of them are blue and the others are red. How many pens are red?
3. If you have 20p, how many 6p sweets can you buy?
4. What is this total? 

5. A cake costs 12p. What change would there be from 20p?

Wizard's Challenge

1 Addition

Grub's up! Add these, while we add more food to our plates.

a 8 + 3 = ☐ **b** 6 + 7 + 4 = ☐ **c** 23 + 5 = ☐

d 17 + 9 = ☐ **e** 50 + 30 = ☐ **f** 40 + 28 = ☐

2 Subtraction

Slurp! Write the answers for these subtractions, while we take a snooze. Use this number line to help.

10 11 12 13 14 15 16 17 18 19 20 21 22 23 24 25 26 27 28 29 30

a 17 – 2 = ☐ **b** 26 – 5 = ☐ **c** 21 – 8 = ☐

d 19 – 14 = ☐ **e** 30 – 27 = ☐ **f** 24 – 18 = ☐

3 Multiplication

Burp! Someone has multiplied the questions! You can do these or we will leave this job for Pointy!

a 

2 + 2 + 2 = ☐ 3 + 3 = ☐

2 × 3 = ☐ 3 × 2 = ☐

b 

5 + 5 + 5 + 5 + 5 = ☐ 5 × 5 = ☐

4 Division

Divide each plate of spiders by 2. Burp!

a 

14 ÷ 2 = ☐

b 

20 ÷ 2 = ☐

c 

18 ÷ 2 = ☐

d 

10 ÷ 2 = ☐

5 Addition and subtraction facts

Write the missing numbers on these tricky trios.

a 7 2 9

7 + ☐ = 9

☐ − 2 = ☐

b 10 6 4

4 + ☐ = ☐

☐ − ☐ = 4

c 3 8 5

☐ + 5 = ☐

☐ − 5 = ☐

6 Times tables

Croak! Hurry up and answer these as quickly as you can.

a 6 × 10 = ☐ **b** 2 × 2 = ☐ **c** 7 × 5 = ☐

d 3 × 5 = ☐ **e** 4 × 2 = ☐ **f** 9 × 10 = ☐

7 Halving and doubling

Now at the double! Answer these.

a Double 4 is ☐ **b** Double 7 is ☐ **c** Double 10 is ☐

d Half of 12 is ☐ **e** Half of 16 is ☐ **f** Half of 18 is ☐

2D shapes

2D shapes are flat shapes. Some have straight sides and some are curved. If you want to be as whizzy as Wizard Whimstaff, try to learn the names of these shapes and be able to describe them.

Count the sides and name the shapes.

To help you name 2D shapes, count the number of straight sides. They each have special names. Super!

Triangles have 3 straight sides.

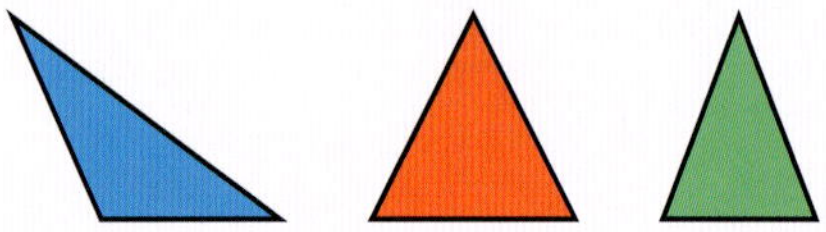

Quadrilaterals have 4 straight sides.

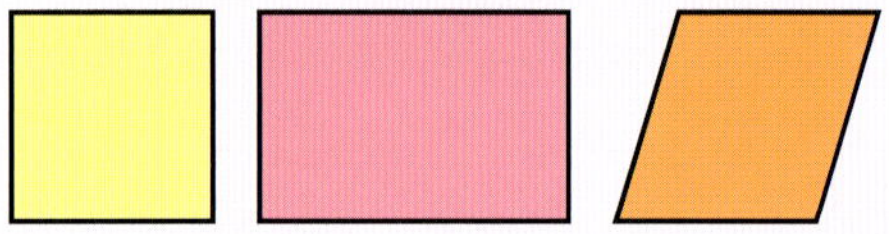

A square has 4 equal length sides.

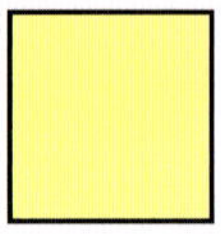

A rectangle has opposite sides of equal length.

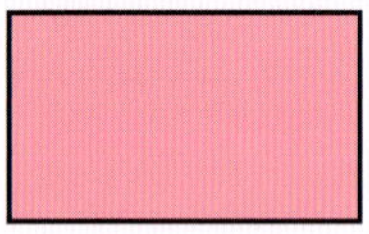

Pentagons have 5 straight sides.

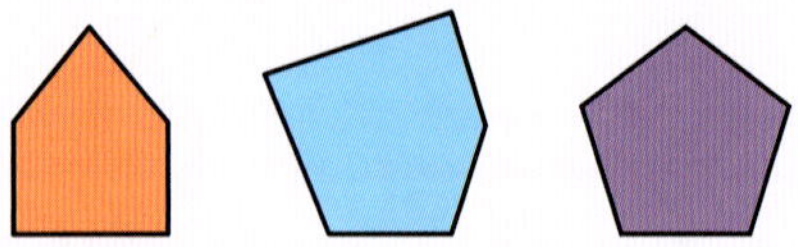

Hexagons have 6 straight sides.

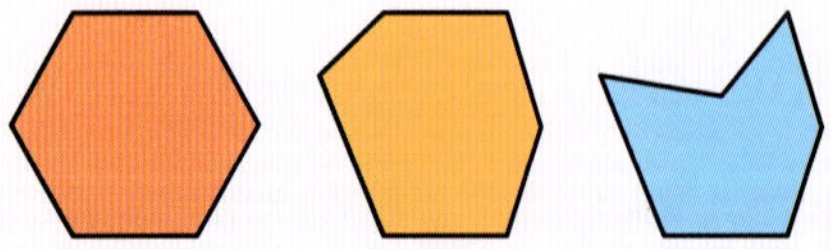

It is useful to remember that some shapes have several different names. A 4-sided shape is called a quadrilateral. Some quadrilaterals are also rectangles and a square is a special rectangle.

Symmetrical shapes look balanced.

Some shapes are **symmetrical**. This sounds like a big word, but it is easy when you know how!

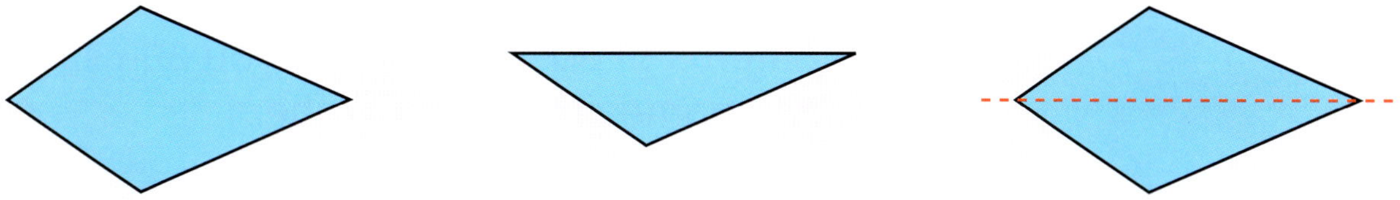

Look at this shape to help you understand it.

This shape is symmetrical. If it is folded down the middle, the two sides would match. That fold line is the line of symmetry and shows that a shape or pattern is symmetrical.

When a mirror is put on the line of symmetry, the half shape and its reflection show the whole shape.

These letters are symmetrical. A D E M

Remember that some shapes are not symmetrical. If they are folded in half, they do not have matching sides.

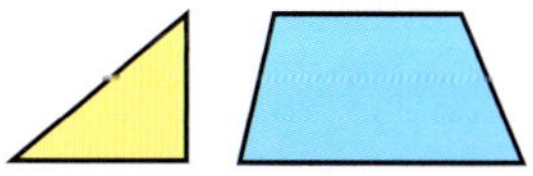

F

MAGIC WORDS
triangle • quadrilateral • square • rectangle
pentagon • hexagon • symmetrical

Wizard's Practice

Workbook pages 32-33

1 Circle the shape that is a hexagon.

2 Name this shape. ______________

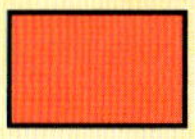

3 How many sides has a pentagon got? ______

4 This shape has been folded in half along the dotted line. If it is opened up, how many sides does it have? ______

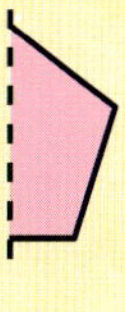

5 Draw a line of symmetry on this shape.

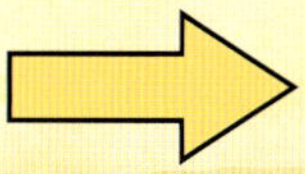

3D solids

3D shapes are all around us, young wizard. Some look the same and some are different. Look for the features of each shape, so you can name and describe them.

Learn the names of solid shapes.

Hey presto! Many 3D solids have special names.

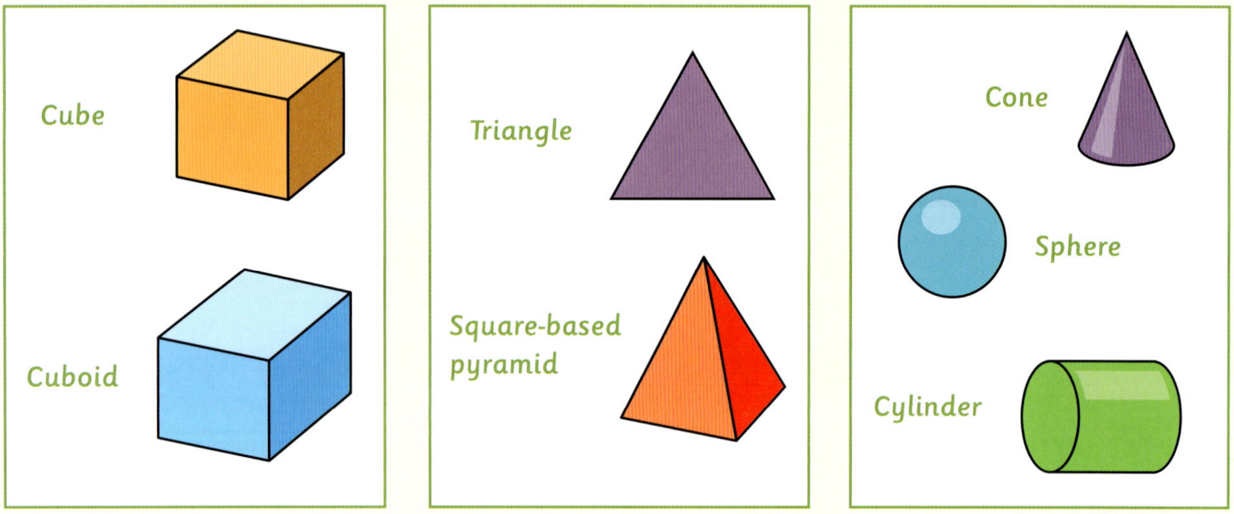

Some shapes are like boxes.

Some shapes are pyramids.

Some shapes are curved.

Try this to help you learn the different shapes.

- Look at one shape and remember its name.
- Close your eyes and picture the shape floating on the back of your eyelids.
- Turn the shape around and try to picture it with different parts facing you.

Learn the properties too.

Allakazan! Solid shapes are made up of **faces**, **edges** and **corners**.

A **face** is a flat surface of a solid.

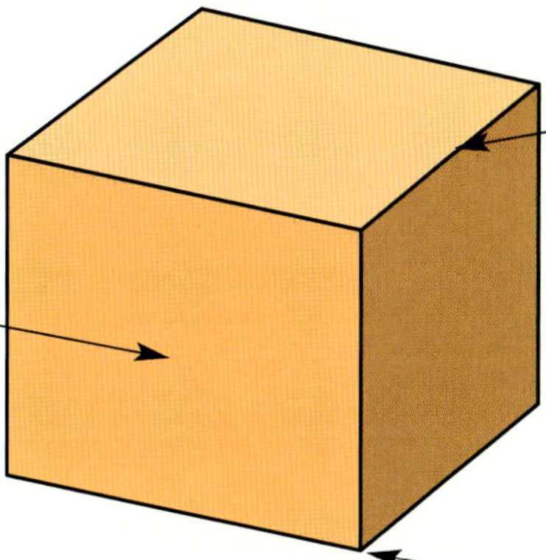

An **edge** is where two faces meet.

A **corner** is where three or more edges meet.

A cube has 6 square faces, 12 edges and 8 corners.

Go on a shape hunt and see how many cubes, cuboids, spheres, cylinders, cones and pyramids you can find.

MAGIC WORDS face • edge • corner

Wizard's Practice

Workbook pages 34-35

1. Name this shape. ______________________

2. Name two solid shapes that have circle faces.

______________________ ______________________

3. What is the name of the shape that is round like a ball?

____

4. How many faces does this shape have? ________

5. Circle the shape that is not a cylinder.

Position and turning

If I turn too much, I get dizzy! Maybe if I learn about turning and direction, it will help me.

Turning one way and the other.

Dabracababra! **Clockwise** and **anticlockwise** are instructions for moving in different directions.

This direction is clockwise.  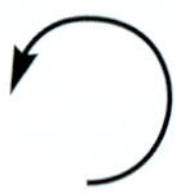 This is anticlockwise.

Quarter-turns, half-turns and whole turns describe how far to turn.

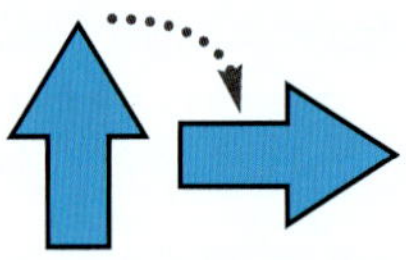

quarter-turn clockwise

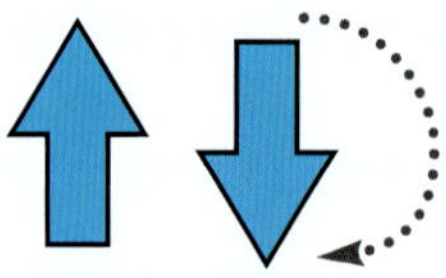

half-turn clockwise

whole turn clockwise

Clockwise moves in the direction of clock hands and anticlockwise goes in the opposite direction.

Right angles are just square corners.

Cabradababa! **Corners** of doors, windows, books and tables all show **right angles**. These 'square' angles are all around you.

A right angle is a quarter-turn, clockwise or anticlockwise.

Squares and **rectangles** have four right angles – one at each corner.

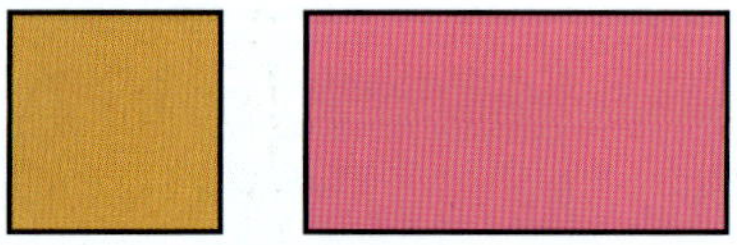

Grids of squares to show position.

A **grid** is useful, because it can show the position of something.

On this grid the star is at D3 and the moon is at B5. Can you see that you read the letter first, then the number, to give the position? You are clever!

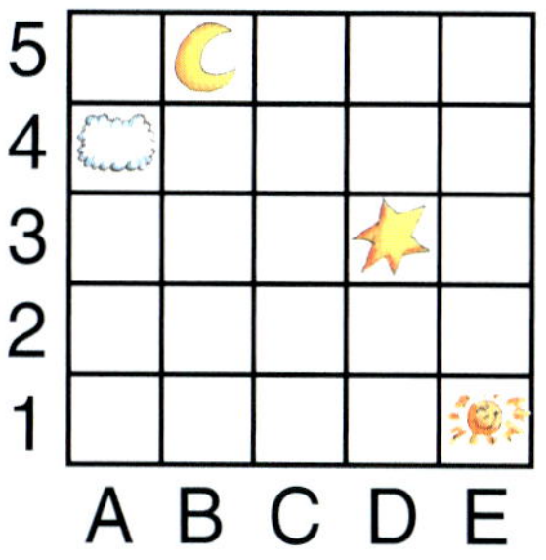

Turning left and right.

Oh dear! I get in a muddle between the two directions, **left** and **right**.

If you face forward, this is left and this is right.

If you cannot remember which is left or right, put your hands like this. Left begins with L, which is the shape of your left hand.

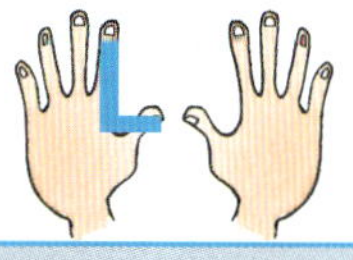

MAGIC WORDS: clockwise • anticlockwise • corner • right angle • square • rectangle • grid • left • right

Wizard's Practice

Workbook pages 36-37

This arrow is pointing to A.

1. Which point will the arrow move to if it makes a quarter-turn anticlockwise? ______
2. Which point will the arrow move to if it makes a half-turn clockwise? ______

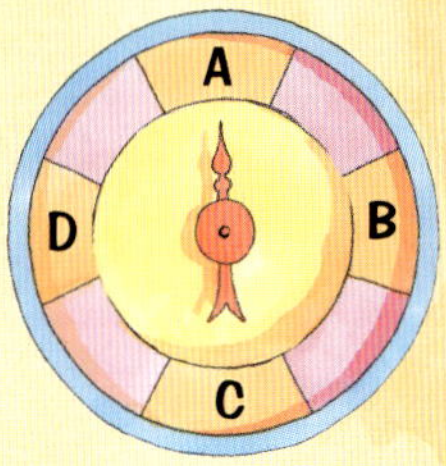

Look at the grid at the top of this page.

3. What is at position A4? ____________________
4. What is the position of the sun? ______

K	L	M	N	O
F	G	H	I	J
A	B	**C**	D	E

Look at this grid.

5. You start on **C**, go up 2 squares, then turn left and go forward 2 squares. Which square do you end on? ______

Measurement

Measurement is great fun! I cannot think of anything better than measuring the length of something, or weighing it or measuring its capacity with a jug. Do not be too messy with food and water, though!

Learn these super units of measure.

Length, **weight** and **capacity** are all measured using different units. Try to learn them.

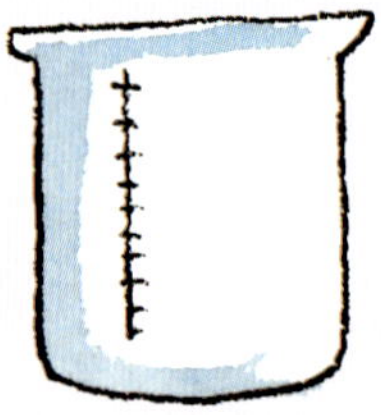

Capacity
1 litre (l) = 1000 millilitres (ml)

Weight
1 kilogram (kg) = 1000 grams (g)

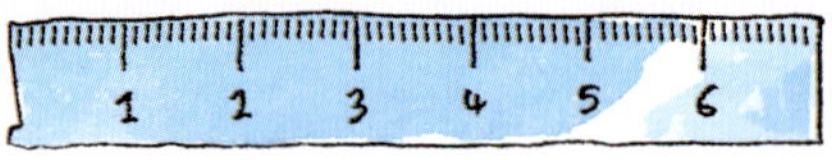

Length
1 metre (m) = 100 cm
1 kilometre (km) = 1000 m

You can use this to work out other amounts. Super!

2 m = 200 cm   3000 g = 3 kg   5 l = 5000 ml

A handspan is about 10 cm long, so use this to work out the length of objects by counting in tens. It is easy when you know how!

Read scales on measuring instruments.

It can be a little bit tricky to read the numbered divisions on a **scale**. Do not worry, you will soon get the hang of it!

Look at the numbers that are written, then the divisions between each number. It is like a number line really, so practise with different number lines.

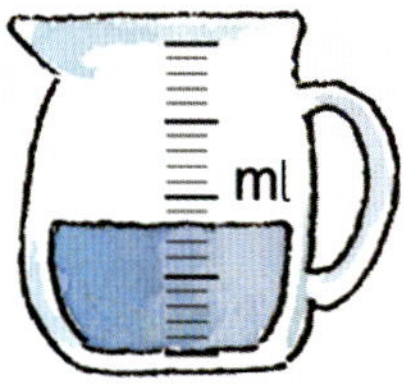

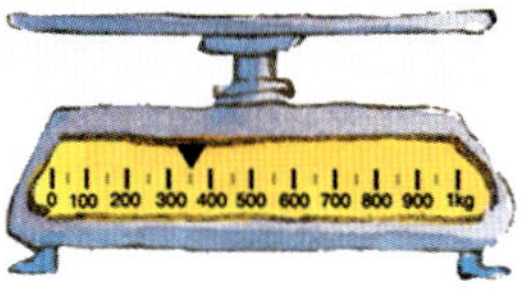

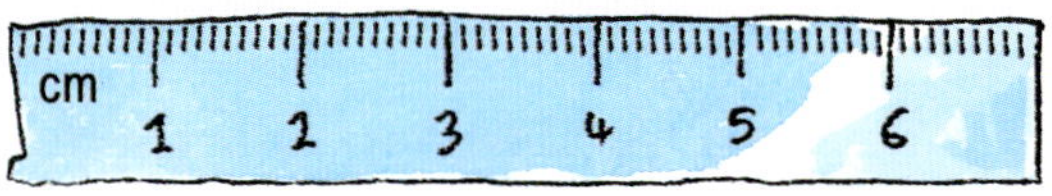

Look at the scales on different instruments we use for measuring.

Length	Weight	Capacity
ruler	dial scales	jug
tape measure	balance scales	spoon
metre stick	spring balance	cup
	floor scales	bucket

Try to get a feel for these weights by holding different objects and 'weighing' them in your hands. 1 gram is a pinch of salt. 20 grams is a teaspoon of sugar. 100 grams is an apple. 1000 grams or 1 kg is a bag of sugar.

MAGIC WORDS: length • weight • capacity • scale

Wizard's Practice

Workbook pages 38-39

1. How many millilitres are there in 2 litres? ________
2. 3 metres = ________ cm
3. What is measured in kilograms: length, weight or capacity? ________
4. What is the length of this line? ________

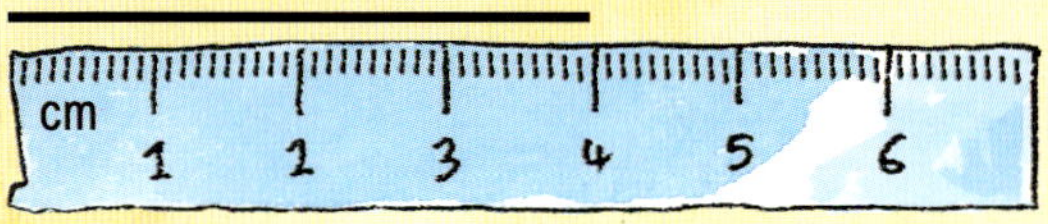

5. How much water is in this jug? ________

Time

Burp! There is never enough time for us to eat all we want. I think minutes should be much longer, then the hours would last for ages!

Time facts – just in time!

Brain cell alert! There are lots of time and **calendar** facts to learn. Cover each one up and see how many you know.

There are 60 seconds in 1 minute.

There are 60 minutes in 1 hour.

There are 24 hours in 1 day.

There are 7 days in a week.

Monday
Tuesday
Wednesday
Thursday
Friday
Saturday
Sunday

There are 12 months in a year.

January
February
March
April
May
June
July
August
September
October
November
December

Slurp! You will need to learn the order of these off by heart.

To help learn the order of the days and the months, keep a **calendar** in your bedroom. Mark off each day on your calendar and you will soon get to know the number of days in each month.

To read the time, just count the minutes past the hour.

Croak! We read the time using these two types of clock. These clocks both show the same time.

a clock with hands

a **digital clock** with the time shown in numbers

The short hand points to the hour, and the longer hand points to the minutes past the hour. This shows 15 minutes past 7.

Just say it as you read it: seven fifteen.

If you find it difficult to read your watch or a clock with hands, then follow these three easy steps.

1. Start with the short hour hand on your clock or watch. Look at the last hour that this hand has gone past. This has gone past the 2, so it is past 2 o'clock.
2. Look at the longer minute hand. Count clockwise around in fives from the top to the hand: 5, 10, 15, 20, 25, 30, 35, 40, 45.
3. Say aloud the hour, followed by the number of minutes. So you would say 2:45, which means 45 minutes past 2.

MAGIC WORDS calendar • digital clock

Wizard's Practice

Workbook pages 40-41

1. What time is shown on this clock? __________

2. A film starts at this time and finishes 1 hour 30 minutes later. What time does the film finish? ________

3. Draw the hands on this clock to match the times.

4. Which month follows September? ____________________
5. How many minutes are there in 2 hours? ____________________

Wizard's Challenge

1 2D shapes

These shapes may all look the same, but one in each set is different to the others. Circle the odd one out. Slurp!

a

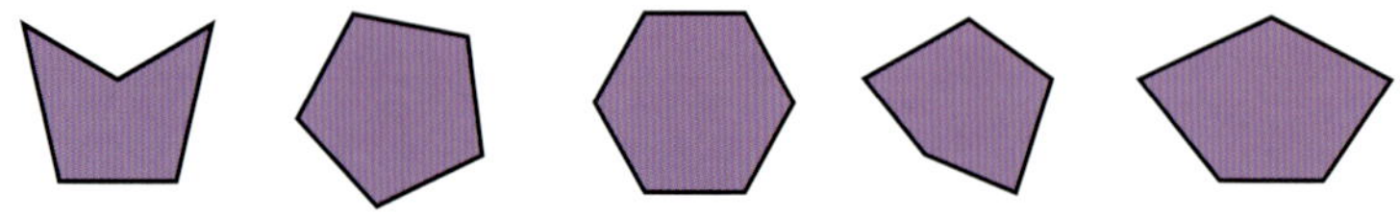

b

c

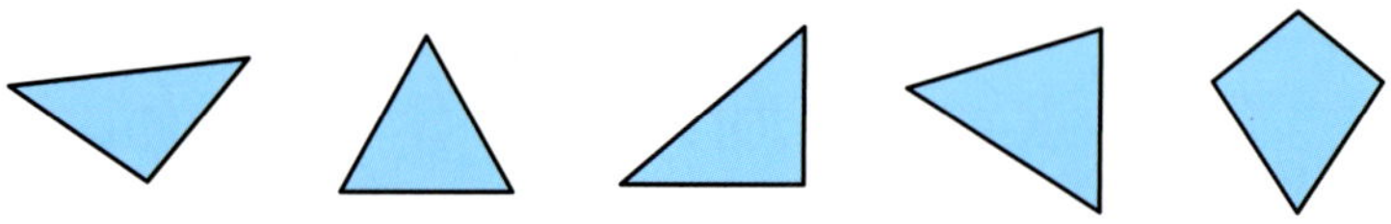

d

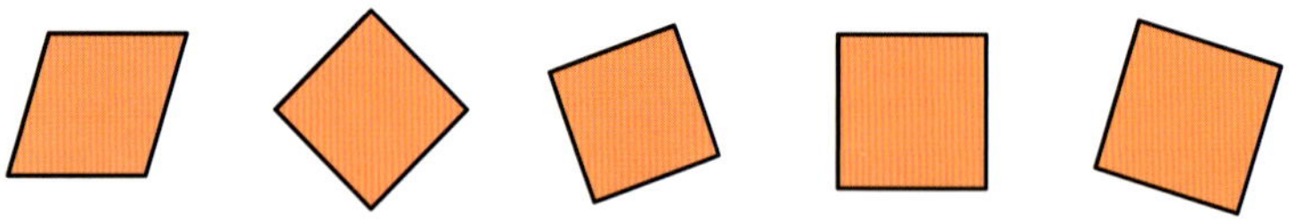

e Can you draw the other half of this picture to make it symmetrical, while we have a snooze? Zzz...

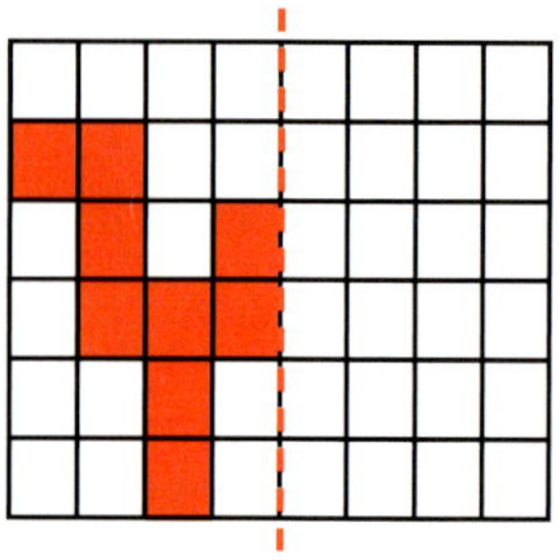

2 3D solids

Join these shapes to their names. Burp!

cube sphere cylinder cone pyramid

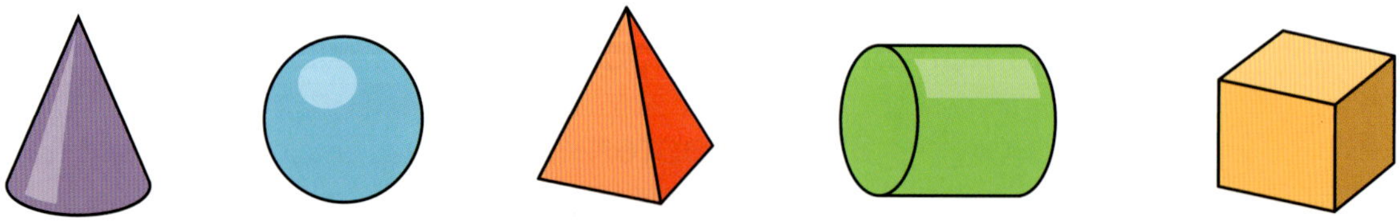

3 Position and turning

a This shape turns $\frac{1}{4}$ turn clockwise. Draw the next shape in this pattern. Sounds like a job for Pointy!

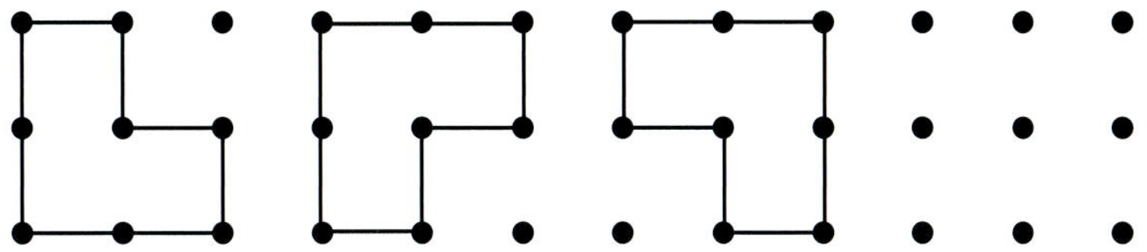

b How many right angles can you see in the shapes above? ☐

4 Measurement

Croak! Join the correct label to each picture.

4 centimetres
4 kilograms
4 litres
4 metres

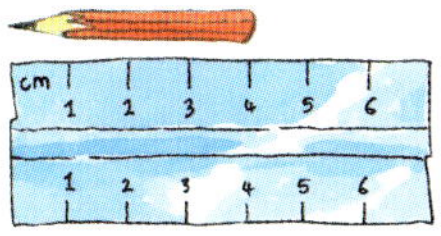

5 Time

a Well done! Now answer this.

A bus left at 8 o'clock to go to the city centre. It arrived 1 hour and 15 minutes later. Draw a circle round the time the bus arrived.

b Grub's up! Fill in the missing months, while we grab a snack.

January → February → ____________ → April

May → ____________ → ____________ → August

September → ____________ → ____________ → December

Lists, tables and diagrams

Let me tell you about lists, tables and diagrams, young wizard. I use them all the time to sort out my spells and you will also find them useful for organising and sorting things.

Allakazan! Lists and tables.

Look carefully at the way these shape **sequences** grow.

Look at the number of counters.

Look at the way the stick patterns grow.

If we really want to see how each pattern grows, we can list the numbers.

Splendid work! Look at the patterns! What do you notice about the numbers in the table?

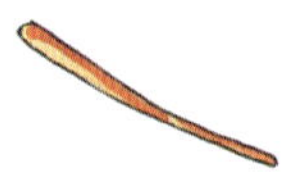	
3	1
5	2
7	3
9	4

Sorting diagrams are good for sorting.

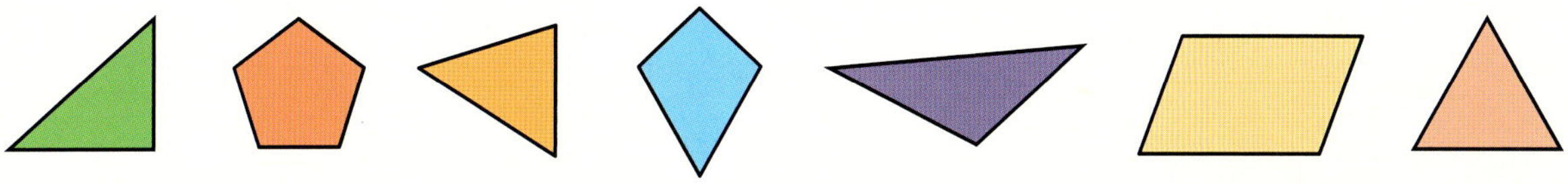

Allakazan! These shapes are all muddled up. I want to sort them so I can find all the **triangles**. I could use either of these diagrams.

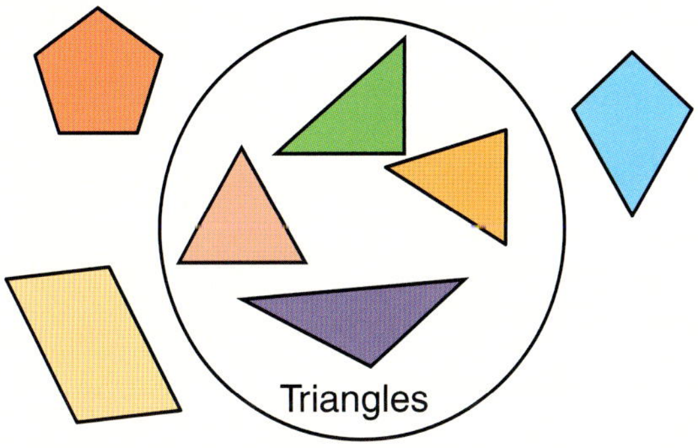

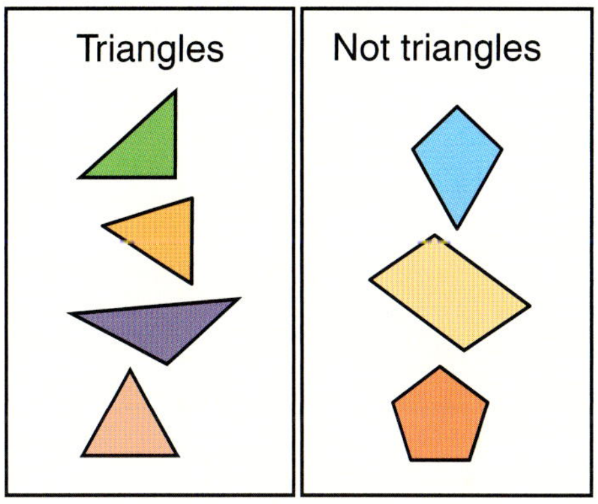

If you have any numbers or shapes to sort, it always helps to have a chart with two columns. Think of a way to sort them into two groups and write headings for the columns.

MAGIC WORDS sequence • triangle

Wizard's Practice

Workbook pages 42-43

These shapes have been sorted.

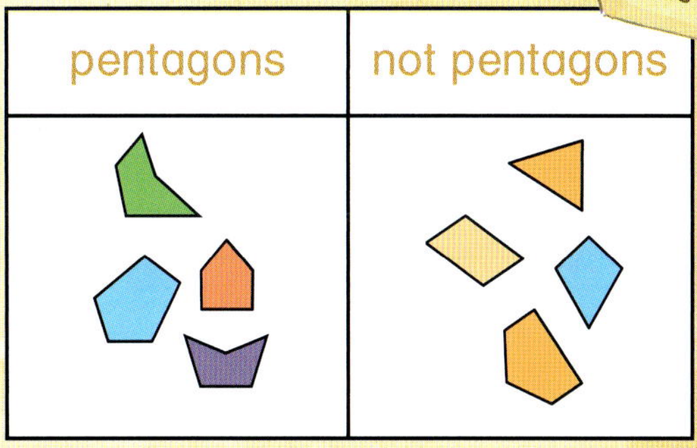

1. Which shape is in the wrong place? Circle it.
2. Draw a hexagon in the correct part of the diagram.
3. These numbers have been sorted. What is special about the numbers outside the circle?

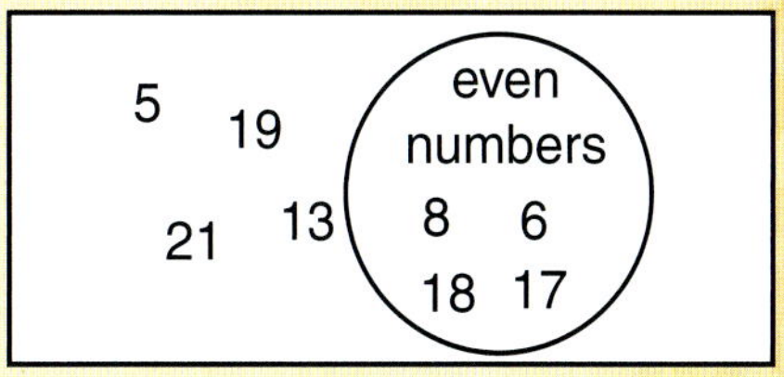

____

4. Write the number 32 in the correct place on the diagram.
5. Write a number greater than 30 outside the circle.

Reading graphs

Count the pictures for pictograms.

Pictograms use symbols or pictures. Each picture stands for a certain number of items. Let's look at an example.

Monday	
Tuesday	
Wednesday	
Thursday	
Friday	

 = 2 bottles

This pictogram shows the number of bottles of potion Wizard Whimstaff uses each day. Each picture stands for 2 bottles.

How many bottles did he use on Tuesday? Did you make it 6 bottles? Oh, well done!

On which day did he use 8 bottles? If you answered Friday, you are very clever!

With pictograms, always look at the key to see what each single picture is showing.

Building up block graphs.

Block graphs or **bar charts** are really clear and simple, because each bar stands for a certain amount. You just have to read all the different parts of the graph carefully.

This graph shows the favourite activities of Mugly and Bugly's friends. As you can see, they are very lazy!

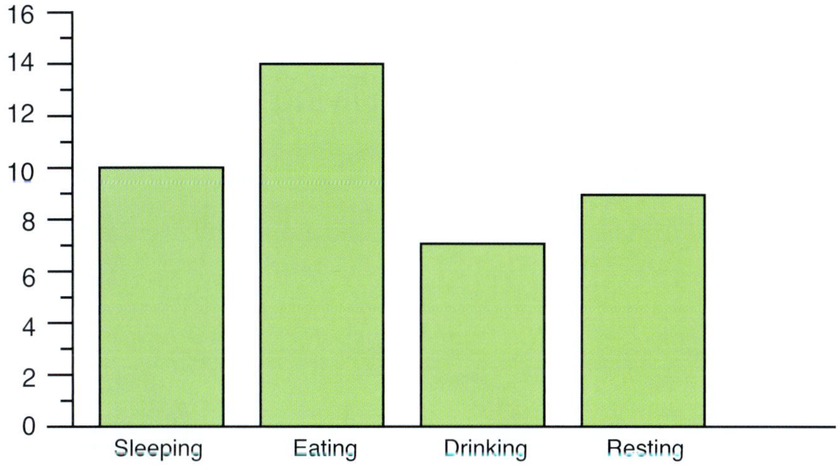

Can you work out how many of them give eating as their favourite activity? Read the numbers carefully to check. Find the bar, go up and then across to the numbers. 14 of them chose eating.

MAGIC WORDS
pictogram • block graph
bar chart

Wizard's Practice

Workbook pages 44-45

Use the pictogram and graph to answer these questions.

1. How many bottles of potion did Wizard Whimstaff use on Monday? ____________________
2. On which day did he use 4 bottles of potion? ____________
3. How many of Mugly and Bugly's friends chose drinking as their favourite activity? ______________
4. Which activity was chosen by 10 of their friends? ________
5. How many more friends chose eating than resting? _______

Wizard's Challenge

1 List, tables and diagrams

a Grub's up! Draw lines from each of these to the correct section on this Carroll diagram.

Living	Non living

b Draw a broom like this in the correct place on the diagram. 

c Draw a spider like this in the correct place on the diagram. 

d Time for a snack! Each one of our frog friends eats 4 bug buns.

Complete this chart to show how many bug buns we need for different numbers of frog friends.

1	4
2	
3	
4	
5	

e We have 4 frog friends visiting today. How many bug buns will they need?

☐

f We have made 12 bug buns. How many frogs will this feed?

☐

2 Reading graphs

Slurp! This graph shows how many hats Wizard Whimstaff has of each colour. Answer these questions while we have a snooze.

a Which colour hat does Wizard Whimstaff have the most of? ____________

b Which colour hat does Wizard Whimstaff have 2 of? ____________

c How many blue hats does he have? ____________

d How many pink and yellow hats does he have altogether? ____________

e How many more green than blue hats does he have? ____________

Brain cell alert! This graph shows the favourite activities of our frog friends. Look at the graph, then answer these questions.

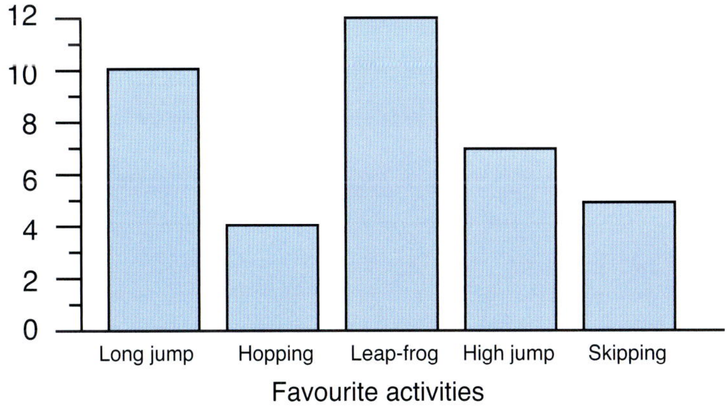

f Which is the favourite activity for 7 frogs? ____________

g How many frogs chose skipping as their favourite activity? ____________

h How many more frogs chose leap-frog than long jump as their favourite activity? ____________

Test Practice

1 Write these numbers in order, starting with the smallest.

21 17 34 14 28 ______________________

2 What is the next odd number after 30? ________

3 Tick the pentagon.

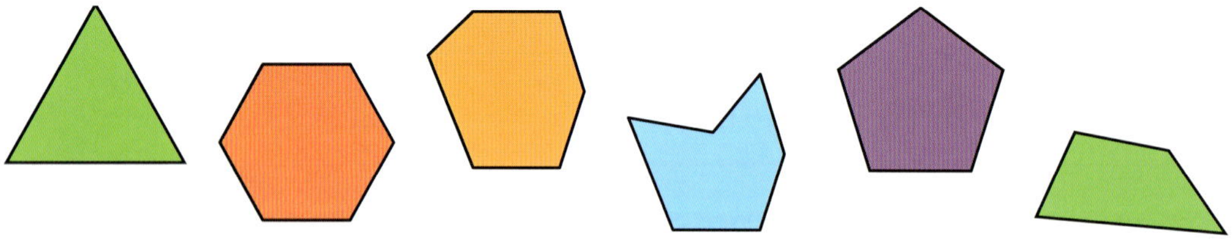

4 A week has 7 days. How many weeks are there in 21 days?

____

5 How much money is in the hand? ________

6 What number is 10 more than 48? ________

7 Which of these angles is a right angle?

a
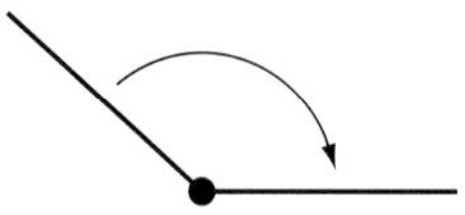

c
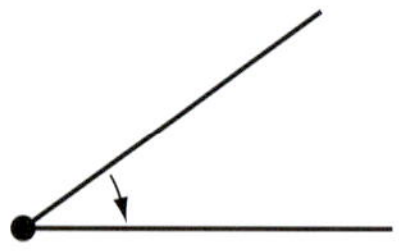

b
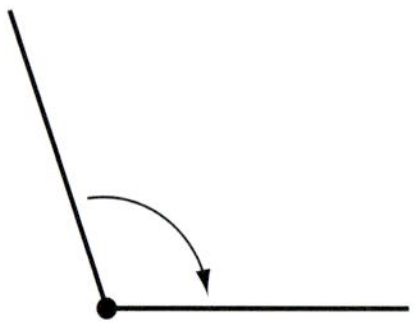

d
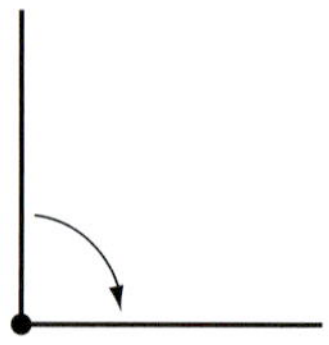

8 14 + 30 = ☐

This graph shows how a group of children travel to school.

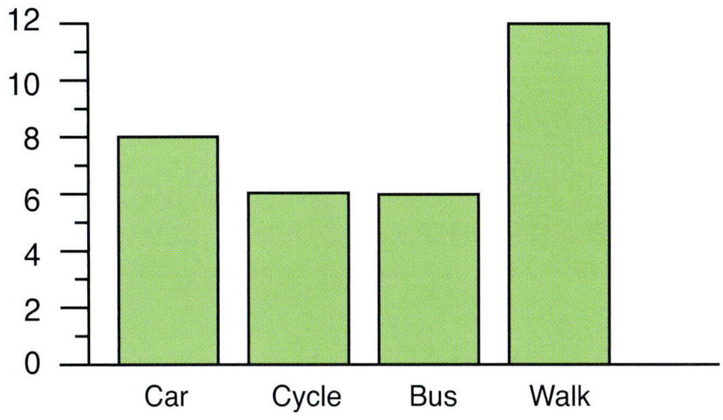

9 How many children travel by bus? ________

10 How many more children walk than travel by car? ______

11 $\frac{1}{2}$ of 18 = ☐

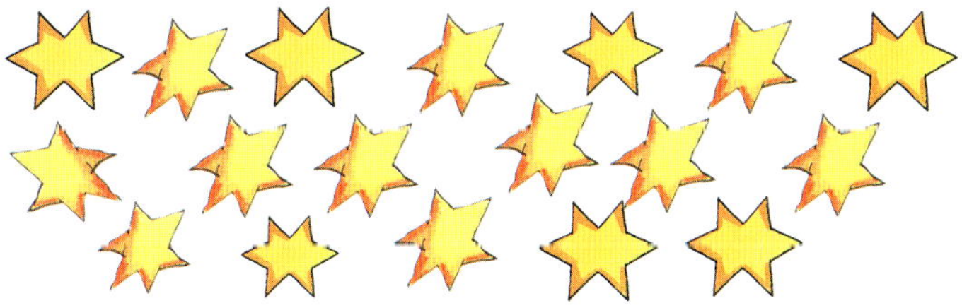

12 What is the missing number in this sequence?

13 15 17 19 ☐ 23

13 Ryan has 50p. He buys a comic for 35p and a sweet for 8p. How much change will he have? ________

14 What is 4 multiplied by 5? ________

15 What is double 15? ________

16 Circle the two shapes that are not symmetrical.

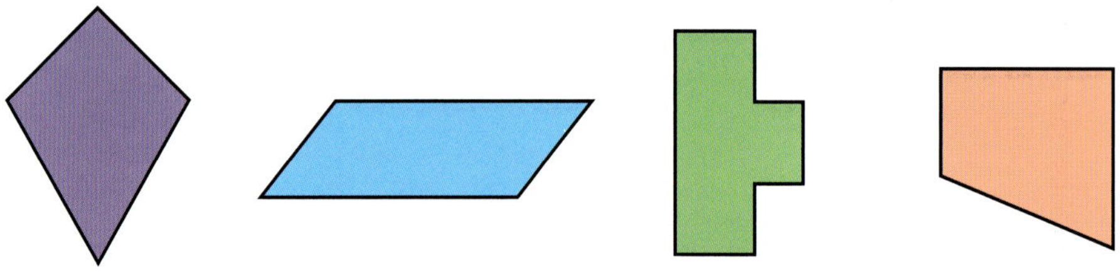

17 Anna needs 14 party bags for her birthday.
The bags come in packs of 5. How many packs
will she need to make sure she has enough bags? ____

18 What is 3 metres in centimetres? __________

19 Shade $\frac{1}{4}$ of this shape.

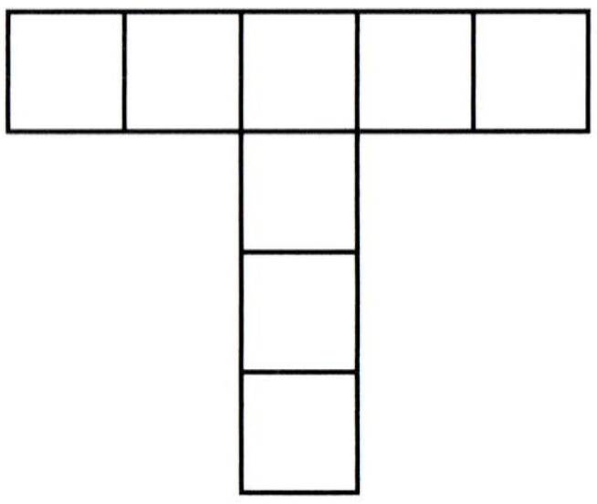

20 What time is shown on this clock? ________

21 What number is 10 less than 47? ________

22 ☐ + 6 = 46

23 Which letter will the arrow point to
if it moves a quarter-turn clockwise? ________

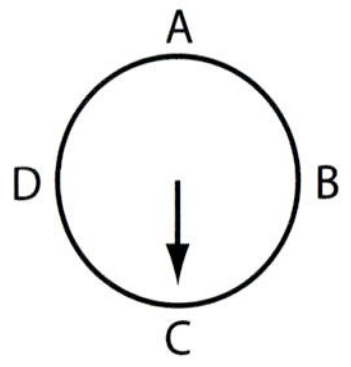

24 Imagine a number line.
What number is halfway between 12 and 20? ________

25 Use one of these signs < or > to make this correct:

34 ☐ 28

26 Estimate the position of the arrow. ________

27 What is 500 cm in metres? ________

28 Dan and Tanya share this money equally. How much do they each get? ________

29 32 – ☐ = 29

30 Circle the three numbers that are not odd.

17 28 15 20 25 14 11

31 Which day comes before Saturday? ________

32 What is the missing number?

20 25 30 ☐ 40 45

33 Place these numbers correctly on this Venn diagram.

16 28 30 42 24 19 31

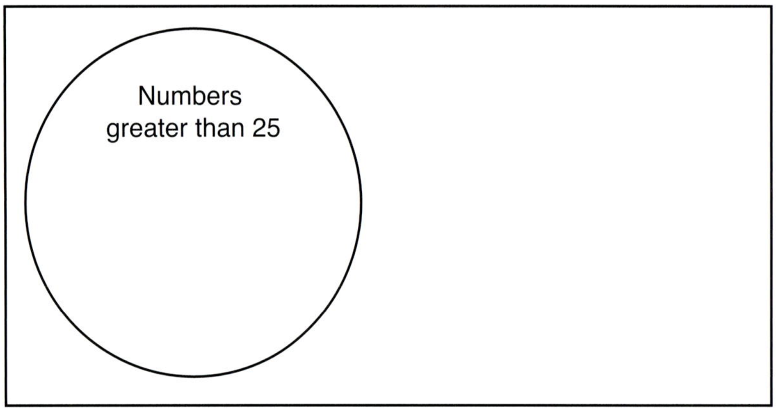

34 There are 10 pencils in each pot and 3 more pencils.

How many pencils are there altogether? ________

35 How much water is in this jug? ________

36 Write a number in the box to make this correct.

3 + 7 = ☐ + 4

37 What is the difference between 18 and 25? ________

38 David puts these apples in bags.

He puts 5 apples in each bag.

How many apples will be left over? ________

39 A cube has 4 red faces and the rest are blue.

How many faces are blue? ________

40 Draw a cross (X) in square C5.

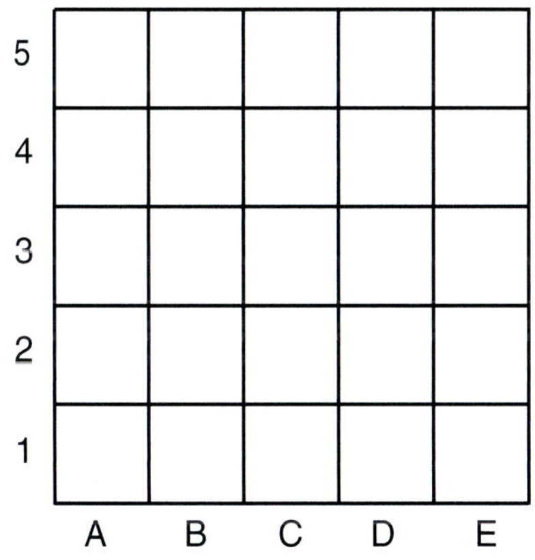

Answers

Page 5

1 Any number between 14 and 18 is acceptable.
2 16
3 17
4 39
5 69

Page 7

1 fourteen
2 18
3 47
4 65
5 48

Page 9

1 odd number
2 even number
3 15
4 11, 24

Page 11

1 red
2 73
3 38 > 19
4 27, 28 or 29
5 18 26 30 34 51

Page 13

1 34
2 61

Page 15

1 $\frac{1}{4}$
2
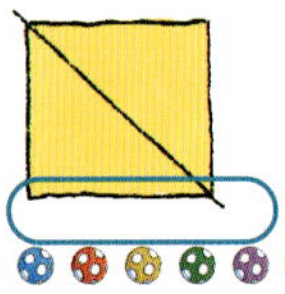
3

4 7
5 5

Pages 16-17

Wizard's Challenge

Actual amounts are:
1 a 8 bugs
b 24 bugs
c 5 bugs
d 15 bugs

2 a 50 + 1 = **51**
b 10 + **9** = 19
c **80** + 2 = 82
d 60 + 3 = **63**

3 a **34** 36 38 **40** 42 44
b 58 59 60 **61** 62 **63**
c 70 **60** 50 **40** 30 20
d 25 28 **31** 34 37 **40**

4 a 97
b 89
c 66
d 93
e 88

5 Estimate near to:
a 5
b 20
c 25
d 40
e 61
f 65
g 70
h 78

6 a 8
b 2
c 5

Page 19

1 16
2 24
3 7
4 70
5 66

Page 21

1 23
2 4
3 30
4 3
5 12

Page 23

1 15
2 3 × 4, 4 × 3 = 12
3 16
4 16
5 15

Page 25

1 4
2 7
3 6
4 5
5 4

Page 27

1 9
2 8
3 2
4 7
5 20

Page 29

1 20
2 16
3 70
4 30
5 18

Page 31

1 14
2 10
3 8
4 8
5 11

Page 33

1 15
2 2
3 3
4 28p
5 8p

Pages 34–35

Wizard's Challenge

1 a 11
b 17
c 28
d 26
e 80
f 68

2 a 15
b 21
c 13
d 5
e 3
f 6

3 a 6
b 25

4 a 7
b 10
c 9
d 5

5 a 7 + 2 = 9 9 – 2 = 7
b 4 + 6 = 10 10 – 6 = 4
c 3 + 5 = 8 8 – 5 = 3

6 **a** 60
b 4
c 35
d 15
e 8
f 90
7 **a** 8
b 14
c 20
d 6
e 8
f 9

Page 37

1 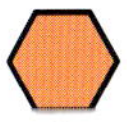

2 rectangle
3 5
4 5
5 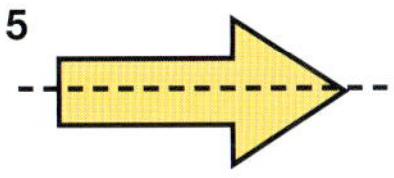

Page 39

1 cuboid
2 cylinder, cone
3 sphere
4 5
5 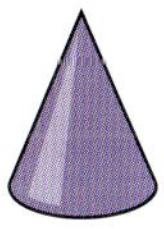

Page 41

1 D
2 C
3 cloud
4 E1
5 K

Page 43

1 2000
2 300
3 weight
4 4 cm
5 $2\frac{1}{2}$ litres

Page 45

1 9.15
2 8.30
3 

4 October
5 120 minutes

Pages 46–47

Wizard's Challenge

1 The odd ones out are:

a 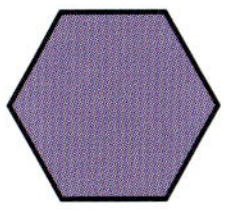

b 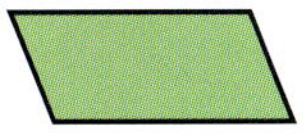

c 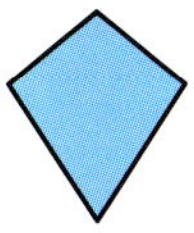

d 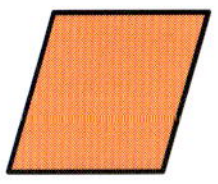

e 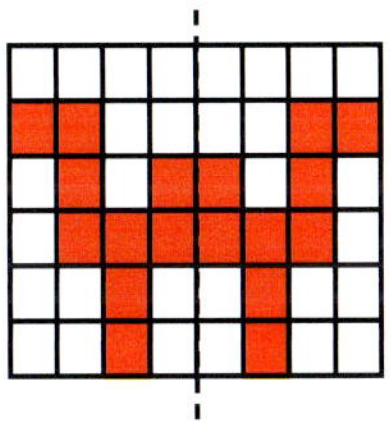

2 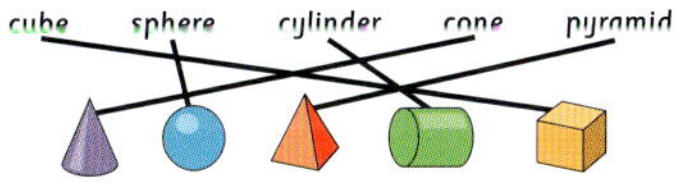

3 a 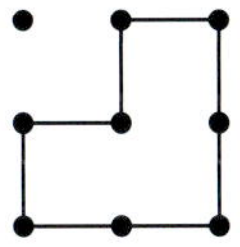

b 24 right angles altogether, 6 on each shape

4 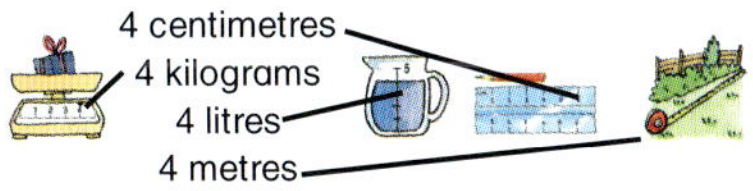

5 a 

b January February **March** April May **June** **July** August September **October** **November** December

Page 49

1 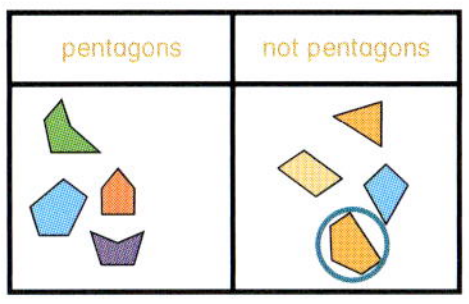

2 Check that hexagon is drawn in the 'not pentagons' column.
3 They are all odd numbers.
4 Check that 32 is drawn inside the circle.
5 Check that an odd number greater than 30 is drawn outside the circle.

Page 51

1 2
2 Wednesday
3 7
4 sleeping
5 5

Pages 52–53

Wizard's Challenge

1 a 

d

1	4
2	8
3	12
4	16
5	20

e 16
f 3

2 a green
b pink
c 5
d 5
e 1
f high jump
g 5
h 2

Pages 54–59

Test Practice

1 14 17 21 28 34

2 31

3 The ticked shape should be:

4 3

5 69p

6 58

7 d

8 44

9 6

10 4

11 9

12 21

13 7p

14 20

15 30

16 Circled shapes should be:

17 3

18 300 cm

19 Any 2 squares should be shaded.

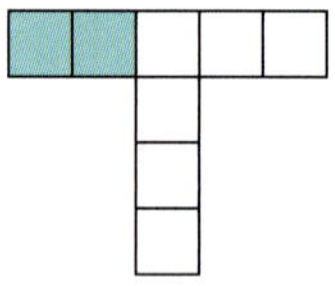

20 4.45

21 37

22 40

23 D

24 16

25 34 > 28

26 15

27 5 metres

28 30p

29 32 – **3** = 29

30 Circled number should be: 28, 20, 14

31 Friday

32 35

33

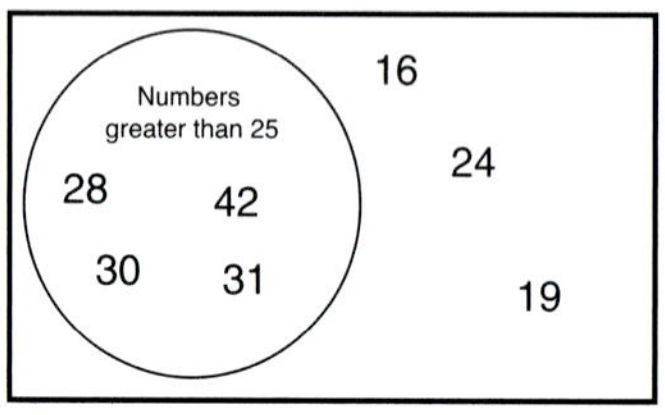

34 43

35 600 ml

36 6

37 7

38 3

39 2

40

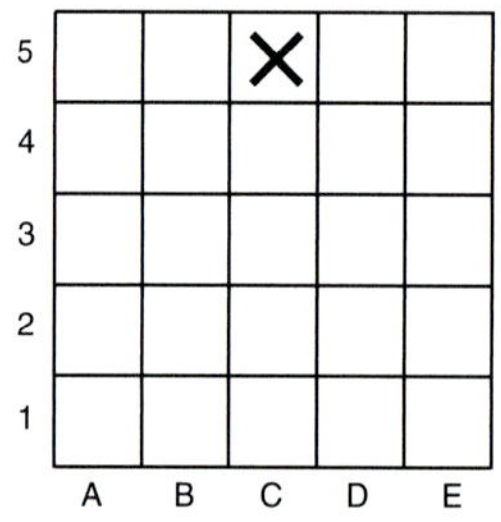

Glossary

anticlockwise a turn in this direction

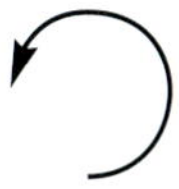

bar chart a type of graph that has bars to show amounts

block graph a type of graph where each block shows an amount

calendar a chart that keeps a record of the days and months through the year

capacity the amount of liquid a container holds

clockwise a turn in this direction

coin the money we use: 1p, 2p, 5p, 10p, 20p, 50p, £1, £2 are all coins

column a column is a line of numbers or objects going up and down, whereas a row goes across from side to side

corner where the edges or sides of a shape meet

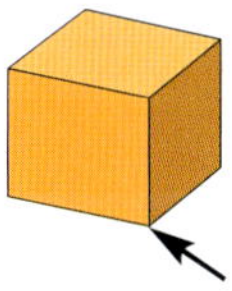

difference the difference between two numbers is the larger number subtract the smaller number. It is often worked out by counting on from the smaller number

digit there are 10 digits: 0, 1, 2, 3, 4, 5, 6, 7, 8 and 9. These digits make up all the numbers we use

digital clock a clock that has a display of numbers, rather than hands

divide to share or group. ÷ is the sign for divide

double to make something twice as big, or multiply by 2

edge where two faces of a solid shape meet

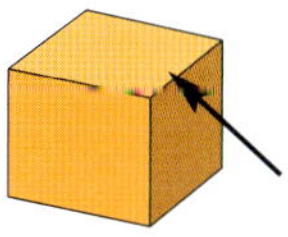

equal when one amount is equal to another, they are the same. The sign is =

estimate a good guess

even number a number that can be divided exactly by 2. Even numbers end in 0, 2, 4, 6 or 8

face the flat side of a solid shape

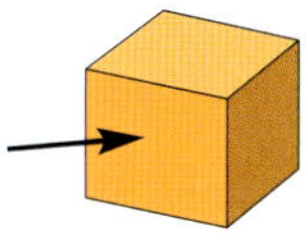

fraction equal part of a whole

grid a set of numbered or lettered squares to help find the position of something

half $\frac{1}{2}$ is one half, or one out of two parts

halve to divide something into two equal parts

hexagon a shape with six straight sides

left this direction is a left turn, which is the opposite of right

length how long an object is – could be measured in centimetres or metres

number bond these are the addition and subtraction facts within 20

odd number a number that cannot be divided exactly by 2. Odd numbers end in 1, 3, 5, 7 or 9

pentagon a shape with five straight sides

pictogram a graph that uses symbols or pictures, where each symbol represents a certain number of items

quadrilateral a shape with four straight sides

rectangle a shape with four sides, with opposite sides of equal length and square corners

right this direction is a right turn, which is the opposite of left

right angle a quarter turn. The corner of a square is a right angle

row a row is a line of numbers or objects going across from side to side, whereas a column goes up and down

scale these are the labelled marks that show an amount on rulers, jugs and weighing scales

sequence a list of numbers which usually have a pattern. They are often numbers written in order

square a shape with four equal sides and four right angles

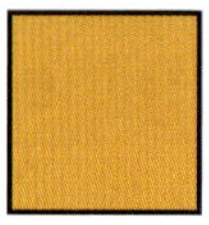

subtract take one amount away from another

symmetrical when two halves of a shape or pattern are identical

total when you add some numbers, the answer is the total

triangle a shape with three straight sides

weight how heavy an object is

zero 0 or nothing